# SHOOTING
## A SEASON OF DISCOVERY

# SHOOTING
## A SEASON OF DISCOVERY

THE DUCHESS OF RUTLAND
WITH JANE PRUDEN

Quiller

First published in the UK in 2012 by Quiller, an imprint
of Quiller Publishing Ltd

British Library Cataloguing-in-Publication Data
A catalogue record for this book is available from the
British Library

ISBN 978 1 84689 146 5

Designed by Tin Can Design Ltd.

Printed in China

## QUILLER

An imprint of Quiller Publishing Ltd
Wykey House, Wykey, Shrewsbury SY4 1JA
Telephone 01939 261616 Fax: 01939 261606
E-mail: info@quillerbooks.com
Website: www.countrybooksdirect.com

# CONTENTS

# FOREWORD

BY HIS GRACE THE DUKE OF RUTLAND

I am delighted that my wife has taken the time to explore the world of shooting game birds, a sport I have enjoyed most of my life here at Belvoir and around the United Kingdom and I have encouraged my five children to shoot. She has set down her observations and thoughts on this valuable pursuit with the help of many of our friends to whom we are very grateful. It is a paradox but shooting birds is integral to the protection of game, wildlife and the preservation of rural pursuits which I and my family treasure and wish to nurture.

Increasing numbers of people realise the importance of game shooting. We welcome more and more people to Belvoir encouraging them to shoot on our estate and stay in our castle. They come to love the countryside and all it has to offer. In times of urban decline and unrest in our cities, our country life offers sanctuary from the daily trials and tribulations and the stresses and strains many have to endure. Greater recognition of our rural inheritance and the need to foster it and preserve it is vital to a balanced society in the future.

May I request all who read this book to group together to defend our sport and way of life. We should enjoy it but be ready to protect it from future encroachments and defend it from those who have sought to denigrate so much else of our national life and tradition.

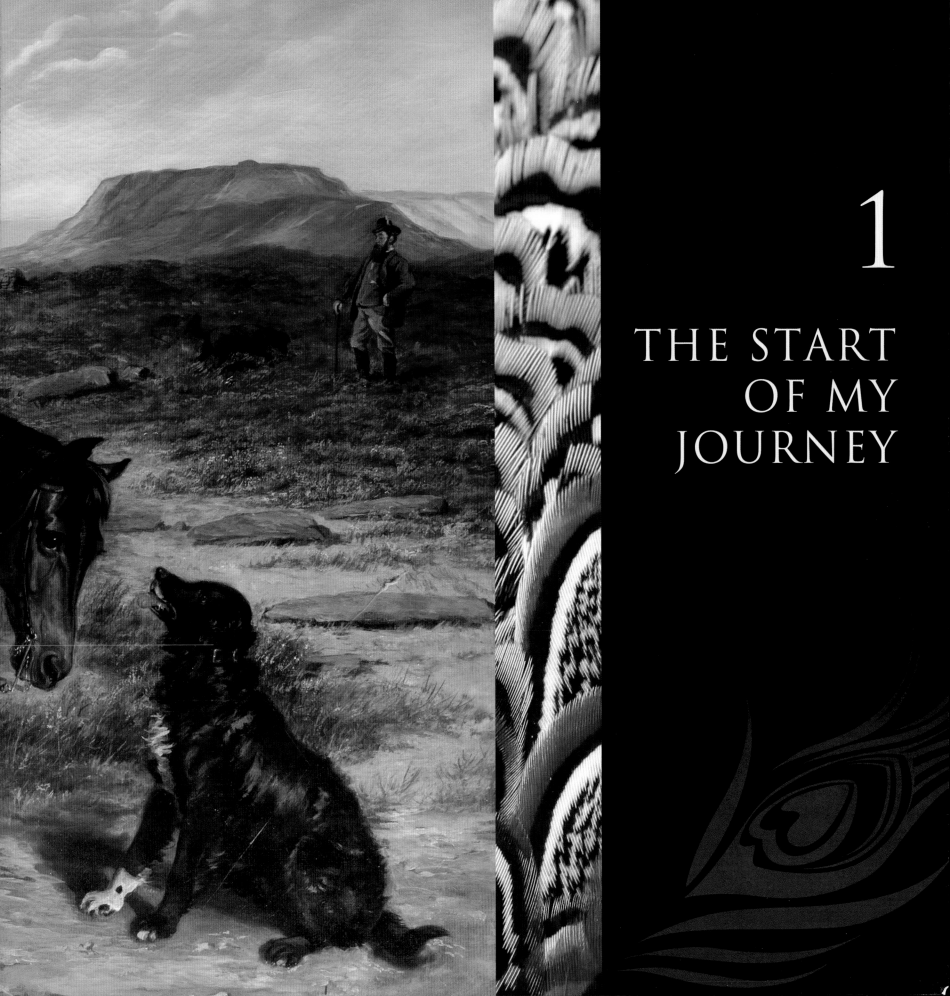

# 1

# THE START OF MY JOURNEY

*Beaters and keepers at Belvoir Castle with many of the family's*
*traditional black retrievers, c.1890.*

I have a clear, early memory of being out shooting, when I was about thirteen. Intensely excited, with my devoted springer spaniel, Janie, at heel, I was proudly beating for my father and his friend Peter. Their shoot was fondly called the 'Rat Patrol' – a tongue-in-cheek euphemism for what almost amounted to poaching. My family's 450-acre farm in Powys, where I was brought up, is sandwiched between two large shooting estates, Stanage Park, now run by Jonathan Coltman-Rogers, and the Harleys' estate, Brampton Bryan. It was always a family joke that although my father, John Watkins, and his great friend, Peter Davies, put some birds down themselves, they invariably shot more than they reared.

My usual role was to help Mum with the organising and cooking. Any dreams I might have had about pulling a trigger myself or rearing birds with my little brothers, William and Roger, were lost, as I cooked sausages for elevenses or cakes for tea. But I was always encouraged to beat, and I loved it. I ran the line with Janie and three other beaters and we took it very seriously. To this day I can still recapture that feeling of exhilaration when my willing dog retrieved her first pheasant from the fast flowing River Teme. The 'Rat Patrol' has moved on but my brother, Willy, still runs a family shoot at home. Nothing has really changed apart from a larger number of poults arriving in the summer, which I'm sure must please his neighbours.

For me, the joy of bagging fifty birds in a day compared to the vertiginous numbers shot at Belvoir was just as intense. Bags of ten birds can, and should, give as much pleasure and be equally as sporting as five hundred.

# THE BELVOIR CASTLE SHOOT

My husband David and I and our five children moved into the castle in 2000, after the death of my dear father-in-law. It soon became clear that its fabulous and historic shoot could be a primary source of income for the estate. Its longstanding reputation placed it amongst the top shoots in the country and, with growing interest in corporate business, it made sense to extend the season with more partridges, refurbish more of the spare bedrooms and invite paying Guns to stay overnight. Our revenue increased dramatically but when the financial crisis struck in 2008 much of the corporate bed-and-

breakfast market, mostly from City firms, withdrew and the shoot's income was slashed by seventy per cent for the 2009 season.

With no time to waste we restructured. We employed the skills of a new shoot captain, Phil Burtt, a local Lincolnshire man who writes a column for *Fieldsports* magazine and whom I had read about in *The Field* magazine's description of the top fifty shots: 'Charming all-round sportsman Burtt receives plenty of awed plaudits from hardened grouse-loaders…' More importantly to us, he knew nearly everyone in the shooting world and had a fat address book stuffed with people who had never shot at Belvoir before and were happy to join us for a day.

In the last twelve years the shoot has grown from eight family and twenty let-days to more than ninety let-days and four for the family. We couldn't do any of it without Phil Burtt or our head gamekeeper, the three full-time beat-keepers, four pickers-up, fifteen to twenty beaters and a small army of dedicated office and house staff.

We are always striving to improve and develop the shoot and present the birds as best we can. Phil constantly reminds us that with over 16,000 spectacular acres there are plenty of areas to experiment with and the forty-five drives are reviewed constantly: should we add more, can we use better cover crops, can we redesign a drive to work better? We never stop trying to improve, like all the dukes have done before David. Their motives weren't always the same as ours and they had different obstacles to overcome but the main objective has never changed – to shoot the best birds at Belvoir.

Scouring the archives for game books, records, letters and diaries to find out about which Dukes of Rutland made their mark, and how, has been hugely informative, not just in understanding our own history but also how national events like the agricultural and industrial revolutions, poaching laws and two World Wars would have shaped other shoots in the country too. I couldn't turn up to all the places in this book to write about my journey of discovery through a shooting season without starting somewhere and Belvoir was the obvious place to begin.

# THE HISTORY OF THE BELVOIR SHOOT

The present castle and the shoot were created at the same time during the affluent Regency era (1795–1837) when large estates across the land were fortified by fortunes from the agricultural and industrial revolutions. Many houses, like Belvoir, were enlarged, enriched and embellished. 'Capability' Brown and Repton parks were maturing. The final Enclosures Act brought woodland, hedges and ditches – a wealth of natural habitat for game. But perhaps one of the shoot's most spectacular assets is a geographic one: the Jurassic escarpment provides the perfect topography for challenging and even stratospheric birds to launch themselves off the Belvoir Ridge.

Stag hunting, the main pastime of every Belvoir Castle occupant since Robert de Todeni was awarded lands by William the Conqueror in 1068, was consigned to history as the landscape changed and deer were enclosed in parkland. There was now fox hunting, made popular by new hedges to jump, technology was producing shotguns, roads were improving for travel and in the age of the *bon ton* country sport was becoming increasingly fashionable.

While shooting wasn't new at Belvoir, by the end of the eighteenth century – the 3rd Duke's 'shotgun' is on display in the Guard Room – the social opportunities it created were. However, while it was fun to kill vermin and game birds for sport, shooting offered more than just frivolous entertainment. For many landowners like the Rutlands shooting was also a journey of discovery, an opportunity to learn about the countryside from gamekeepers and estate staff at ground level. They learned about the changing agricultural landscape,

modern farming methods and its effects on wildlife. Respect for your quarry is the recurring theme of Belvoir's early game books – though there is a lot of competitive spirit there too!

The seeds of the decadent sporting house party, that lasted well into the twentieth century, were being sown and every aristocrat worth his acres revelled in the incessant round of sporting activity.

In 1800, the 5th Duke of Rutland was twenty-two and recently married. Yet despite the demands of his military career, the need to rebuild his castle, his London social life and many days spent hunting, still he managed to shoot almost daily in the season.

Along with family and friends he would journey to his grouse moor near Hawnby in North Yorkshire for the Glorious Twelfth for a week. His intimate parties of four or five guests, at Bumper Castle on the moors, would shoot in the region of 400 grouse in good years.

He liked to send a brace to his wife, Elizabeth, wherever she might be holidaying, and wrote to her in 1803[1]: 'I have thought it best to order only a leash of brace of birds to be sent to Ramsgate; as the weather is very hot and they will not travel well... I am fearful they will not arrive sweet.' Poor Elizabeth wrote to him the following year, this time from Brighton, '... and do not send me any more grouse for I think it is impossible it can come sweet'. I love to think of the young duchess in the first flush of married life, staying with their two tiny infants at her chic seaside resort and receiving all these disgusting grouse, which had travelled at least 300 miles over two days, sweating in a stagecoach – and not knowing how long to leave it before begging her dear husband to desist!

*Opposite Page*
*John Henry Manners, 5th Duke of Rutland, c.1794–96, by John Hoppner. The young duke's passion for shooting lasted all his life.*

**1**  *The private letters of the 5th Duke and Duchess of Rutland in the Belvoir Archives*

The grouse shooting days started at seven o'clock in the morning and the party would not return before eight in the evening for dinner. They schlepped over the moor for miles. The duke wrote[2]: 'Shelley (Sir John Shelley Bart) is the most bloody-minded fellow you ever saw, he is never content with meandering, and while there is a grouse left he would slave ten miles in order to kill him.'

After the excitement of the grouse moor the Duke travelled south to another family estate, Cheveley Park, near Newmarket in Suffolk, to shoot partridges for a couple of months. The parties were bigger, grander and with guests like Beau Brummell and the Duke of York, probably wilder too.

Despite being an enthusiastic and top-class shot, frequently bagging the most birds, shooting at Belvoir did not feature much in the Duke's early letters. He shot birds and ground game almost every day with a keeper and sometimes with a brother or visitor but it's possible that this was such an everyday occurrence that it failed to inspire him sufficiently to write about it.

Poaching was a problem that did incite correspondence, however, and on 23 December 1831, the 53-year-old 5th Duke of Rutland wrote to D'Ewes Coke, his agent at Bakewell for the Haddon Estate, 'The new Game Act has multiplied poaching here. The whole of the labouring population seems at work to supply the markets...'[3] The Game Reform Act, 1831[4] tightened some closed seasons, reduced penalties for insubordination and more pertinently allowed people to shoot who had previously been unqualified. From 1389[5] the law had stated, to varying degrees, that you

In the late 1890s, a wonderful
game cart on the Longshaw
grouse moor.

could only shoot if you owned lands or tenements to a particular value, ergo shooting was the preserve of the landed gentry and aristocracy. In addition, you could only be a JP if you qualified by the same rule. Hearings, while not always completely biased, did tend to be prejudiced and as such stimulated further unrest.

Poaching represented more than criminality: it was, for many, a fight for a fairer society. Added to which many labourers returning from the Napoleonic Wars found little work. Poaching both fed and provided income – at a price. Game was there for the taking and increasing numbers of people across the nation took their chances with the law. In 1816, 868 poachers were convicted. By 1820 the figure was 1,467[6]. Many of those convicted in the 1820s were unable to pay their fines and were imprisoned. Game had fetched good prices on the black market as middle-class industrialists aspired to live – and eat – like the gentry. But poachers soon became victims of their own success; game flooded the market and prices plummeted. Once a poacher had been able to pay his fine from his takings and return home, but increasingly his booty was worth less than the penalty. Gamekeepers were being caught up in violent conflicts too and the whole situation was untenable and out of control.

The 5th Duke opposed reform. He had great sympathy for the poor and had worked hard to support poorer families on the estate but he believed the Game Bill would not reverse immorality in those intent on theft and violence. He wrote on 18 January 1832 to Lady Shelley (wife of Sir John Shelley, one of the great opposers of the bill, like the Duke of Wellington): 'As for

2  ibid

3  ibid

4  Gentlemen and Poachers P. B. Munsche

5  ibid – To keep dogs or to use ferrets, nets or other 'engines' to take deer, hares, conies, or 'other gentleman's game'

6  Gentlemen and Poachers P. B. Munsche

*Young Guns: E. Manners and G. Manners preparing for a day out in 1881.*

*The 7th Duke of Rutland's keepers and beaters at Longshaw Moor.*

the new Game Bill, it will eventually put down poaching by leaving no game in the country to poach. There has been a great increase in the poaching tribe since the Act was passed, and it is a farce to suppose that when there is nothing more to poach those men will take to honest living. The whole Act is based on a false philanthropy.'[7]

He would have had ample opportunity to discuss politics during his infamous sporting birthday parties. His wife, Elizabeth, had always hosted wonderful celebrations for him and after her death in 1825 he continued the tradition. Charles Grenville wrote in his diary: 'All the men hunt or shoot.'[8] But it is curious that the records for both shooting days that weekend list the Duke of Wellington, Prince Esterhazy, the Austrian ambassador, Charles Grenville, Mr Arbuthnot and Lord Salisbury as guests, and yet only the Duke appeared to shoot anything.

By the mid-nineteenth century, before the 5th Duke died in 1857, the Belvoir shoot was in full swing and regularly bagging about 1,800 head of game a season. Records often show a higher number of partridge than pheasant shot during these years and nearly as many hares and rabbits as pheasants. The driven shoot, both at Belvoir and other estates, had been established and his old friend, the Duke of Cambridge, brother to the late King George IV and the Duke of York, was a regular visitor, often staying at Belvoir until his death in 1850.

The 6th Duke, like his father, was a passionate sportsman. Bumper had been sold along with many other smaller Rutland estates to pay for castle rebuilding costs but he shot grouse at Longshaw Moor on the Haddon Hall estate. He was an excellent host, holding parties most weekends for hunting and shooting. European royals and the Prince of Wales were guests at

Belvoir and Cheveley. Big bags were an essential requisite on such visits. By many other estates' standards, which could produce bags of up to 4,000 a day, Cheveley was small-fry but the Prince of Wales and his brother, the Duke of Edinburgh, shot 1,200 birds in two days at Herringswell on the Cheveley estate in 1881. The 6th Duke shot right up until his death in March 1888 and the Belvoir game book records his last day shooting ground game on the 6 February 1888, 'This was the last occasion on which the Duke of Rutland was able to shoot.' He stopped after a cracking year: 2,242 pheasant, 789 partridge, 1,843 rabbits and 1,206 hares.

A period of average shooting activity took place during the 7th Duke's occupancy: he was a politician and preferred his books and his fishing but his sons and friends shot regularly. Family friend Sir Edwin Landseer, with whom he worked on the placement of the lions in Trafalgar Square when the duke was Lord Derby's First Commissioner of Works, stayed with the Rutlands at Haddon. We found some delightful sketches that we think he must have done on a visit to Longshaw Moor. The most significant change to the family's shooting diary during this time was the sale of Cheveley in 1893 because it was costing too much to run.

Though the 8th Duke was a keen shot, in 1908 he was forced to make economies too and he let out a trial syndicate shoot to his neighbours, the Earl of Dysart and a Mr Pryor. He had had meetings with his London solicitors, Eyre and Dowling 9, and it is likely that they encouraged him to look at ways of increasing the estate's revenue. Letting out the odd beat wouldn't earn a fortune but it might start to offset some of the family's shooting expenses at Belvoir. What is more his wife, Violet, had ambitious plans to install electricity

7  *The Diary of Frances Lady Shelley, 1818–1873 Edited by Richard Edgcumbe*

8  *The Diaries of Charles Greville Edited by Edward Pearce*

9  *Private letters of the 8th Duke in the private family archives*

and a raft of bathrooms in the castle, and death duties, introduced in 1898, were also crippling the accounts. By 1915, the Duke was back at his solicitors to discuss finances and wartime taxation. It was decided to extend the offer of shooting rights and the syndicate shoot was launched.

The first terms of agreement allowed Mr Pryor of Egerton Lodge in Melton Mowbray the use of 3,620 acres, including Croxton Park, which still had a small deer park (though this was soon to be phased out). The conditions stipulated that the numbers of rabbits and hares had to be kept down within the season and there was also a concession to farmers 'upon whose land most game is killed and whose land adjoins woods, to be liberally treated as to game'[10]. This would have been a cautionary as well as a respectful gesture, for many people would still remember both the effects of the agricultural depression and of the poaching wars before and after the Game Act in 1831. Syndicates were also obliged to leave sufficient numbers of birds to breed through the spring and summer. An annual charge of £200 covered the head keeper, Mr Dent's, fees but the £20 a year for each beater, sundry expenses and the costs of the keepers' dogs all had to be settled with Mr Dent directly.

During the First World War regular deliveries of game were made to both local and London hospitals. The Duchess was running a convalescent hospital for officers at the family's London home in Arlington Street and her daughter, Lady Diana, was working as a nurse. Diana's friends and husband-to-be, Duff Cooper, are all listed in the game books and shot regularly at Belvoir during the season.

In 1919, records show the estate making £824 from letting and transactions with game dealers: a healthy contribution towards offsetting the shoot expenses of £1,260.

There was no shortage of takers for the shooting at Belvoir amongst local residents, tenant farmers and businessmen from Nottingham and Leicester all keen to shoot there, well disposed as they were at the time to a day trip with the advent of the motorcar. But poor Mr Dent clearly had his work cut out with poachers if his poem, written on 9 February 1932, is anything to go by. Although long, it is so illustrative of 'the chase', that it is reproduced in full overleaf. You can almost hear his heart thumping in places!

*Above*
*Our youngest son, Hugo,*
*receiving instruction on our*
*family day.*

*Right*
*Alice under the supervision of big John.*

*10 Private documents in the Belvoir Archives*

# THE CAPTURE OF DISNEY

One night when the winds from the West
    howled strong:
And the moon high up was gleaming
'Twixt clouds, neither roll-roll-rolled along
O'er the Heath; where Fred lay dreaming.

Now Fred had chance of the game up there.
And game there was – all teeming
The partridge, pheasant, rabbits and hare
And the Plovers now, were screaming.

Well, Fred he dreamed he heard a shot
And he dreamed of the Plovers' warning.
With a start – he woke – alert and hot
'Twas now, two o'clock in 'a morning

With him, was Joe, his faithful chum
Both wearied out through watching
For the Disney Gang who would sure to come
And who they knew would take some catching

Now Disney hailed from Nottingham town
And his life of crime was appalling
To poach – to thieve – and rough up and down
Appeared to be his calling

Strong built was he, and hefty too
Agile and full of cunning

With gun he'd turn and threaten you
When he was beat at running

As the Keepers crowded in the shade of a nook
With ears and eyes a'streaming
They saw a flash and heard a crook
So on they crept – a'gaining

On tiptoe down the covert stride
All eager now – heart thumping
They saw two shadows on the ride
Now soon, there'll be some thumping.

At last some stubby old Black Thorn
With briar intertwining –

Held Disney fast – his clothes were torn
Both outside – and the lining

There Fred, delighted in his gains
And victory loud proclaiming
Stood back – for Disney at his brains
His gun was truly aiming

But Joe was young, and Joe was quick
And Joe was full of daring
He slipped behind and with his stick
Upset poor Disney's bearing

Then down they all went in a heap
The trio all uniting
And in a rolling ball did keep
And did some rough in-fighting

At last poor Disney had enough
And for mercy loud beseeching –
He slackened off, quite out of puff –
All energy decreasing.

And so it was, they walked him off
While the wild wind still was howling
This king of crime,– this poacher Toff –
For a' time, will cease his prowling.

*Above*
*Roy discussing tactics with the Duke*

It would be lovely to know who Disney was but Fred was Fred Tinkler, the keeper, and Joe, Tinkler's assistant. The whole poem is such a wonderful evocation of a lost time: poaching a rabbit or pheasant is not so common these days. Mr Dent wrote a lot of poetry and he carefully stuck many of his rhymes in the game book.

By the 1930s a new generation of royalty was enjoying the pleasure of Belvoir's topography. The Duke of York, later King George VI, was a guest of my husband David's grandfather, the 9th Duke. Like his ancestors at Cheveley in 1881, the royal visitor was amongst the Guns who shot one of the biggest bags of the decade at Belvoir on 24 November 1932, totalling 742.

Probably one of the most riveting shooting weekends is recorded on 13 December 1936 in the game records and visitors' books. The day before had provided a defining moment in history, of the type that stops everyone in their tracks and everyone remembers where they were when they heard the news: Edward VIII's abdication. The announcement resonated very deeply at Belvoir. Winston Churchill and his wife, Clementine, were due to stay for a shooting party but the constitutional crisis had been threatening to explode all week and reached its climax on the first night of the house party. King Edward VIII had been forced to relinquish the throne, despite many attempts by himself and a posse of supporters, including Churchill, to prevent the inevitable.

Churchill arrived too late to shoot, but whatever the reason he missed Belvoir's all-time record bag of 1,189 of winged game.

David's grandfather had been expecting to shoot on 3 September 1939 but as Neville Chamberlain's declaration of the outbreak of war was broadcast to the nation at 11.15am, the duke put down his gun. Retired keepers kept things ticking over for family days and the syndicates kept shooting but rearing was banned through the war and for a few years afterwards. As before, game was sent to hospitals and across the country for Christmas presents as a measure of goodwill.

*We encourage all the youngsters to have a go and we are fortunate to have some very able instructors to help them.*

My father-in-law, Charles, the 10th Duke, was only twenty when he succeeded to the dukedom in 1940 and was serving as a subaltern in the Grenadier Guards.

Retired head keeper, Ron Wells, whose father, Colin, was head keeper before him from 1959, recalls stories from the 1940s to the late 1970s. Farming had changed fundamentally after the war and the effects of this were felt on the shoot. A lot of small tenant farms on the estate merged into bigger units, resulting in the steady loss of small fields of roots for sheep that had once provided cover for game too. In addition there were fewer people keeping chickens meaning there were less broody hens to hatch and rear partridge and pheasant chicks. As for the actual shooting: partridges were driven mostly off open stubble fields or root crops and pheasants were shot out of traditional woodland, which had been regularly planted from the 1870s onwards on the hilltops so as to show the birds at their best. In the 1960s and 1970s the family shot about nine days and averaged 5,000 heads of winged game a season. By the late 1970s commercial shooting was developing across the country and estates, including Belvoir, were keen to market their potential but this meant more changes.

Cover crops and even more trees were planted to create twice as many drives, whilst incubators and brooders were bought to rear chicks. But it all took time to establish, especially the rearing: incubator instructions were fairly basic by all accounts and success was a matter of trial and error. Disease in chicks and young birds caused a lot of problems too. But eventually a sufficient number of birds, including red-leg partridge, were produced on the estate to secure a manageable, but not overly commercial, business from the shooting. Then, as I said at the beginning of this chapter, everything changed again to become the commercial shoot that we run at Belvoir today.

*Left*
*Esmie Bertilson retrieving a bird*
*on a family day.*

*Above*
*As far as anyone can remember it*
*has been a family tradition to*
*finish every shoot with a duck*
*drive on the bridge over the lakes.*

# THE ESTATE'S BIO-DIVERSITY

Natural England, the government's advisers on natural environment, helps many farmers and landowners with stewardship and payment schemes and the Entry Level Stewardship scheme (ELS) has assisted us with many of our achievements over the last five years. One of our priorities has been to enhance the estate's natural resources to increase its bio-diversity which, as an added advantage, also benefits the shoot and its intrinsic ecological value. We have recently applied for acceptance to the Higher Level Stewardship scheme and we will find out in 2012 if we have been successful.

Over a proposed ten-year period the HLS would protect and maintain many of the landscape features on the estate: built water features, three Sites of Special Scientific Interest (SSSIs), an area of species rich grassland and two further areas of SSSI wood pasture (parkland); ponds rich in biodiversity that are of Biodiversity Action Plan (BAP) habitat quality, stone walls and hedgerows of high environmental value, ancient trees and lowland meadows. The combined ELS and HLS schemes would also support the shoot with sympathetically positioned wildlife seed mixes, nectar flower mixes, floristically enhanced grass margins and cultivated fallow plots.

The wild bird populations would all flourish too. A recent RSPB bird survey and Farm Environmental Plan (FEP) inspection established that the estate also plays host to several key species of farmland birds. Evidently, we have significant numbers of bird species of high and medium conservation concern, such as skylark, yellowhammer, house sparrow, yellow wagtail, song thrush, linnet, marsh tit, starling, bullfinch, buzzard, dunnock, green woodpecker, kestrel, red kite, lapwing, mistle thrush, reed bunting, stock dove, sparrowhawk, tufted duck and willow warbler. We are very keen to make sure that we are doing everything we possibly can to conserve and hopefully increase their numbers here.

In 2009 we started a five-year project to reverse the decline of some of the region's woodland birds. The Forestry Commission's Woodland Bird Scheme and the RSPB are carrying out a sustainable management programme on approximately 250 hectares of our woodland. The RSPB are targeting sixteen endangered species in the East Midlands and they hope that nine of them – the marsh tit, willow tit, lesser spotted woodpecker, woodcock, lesser redpoll, redstart, wood warbler, willow warbler and hawfinch – will benefit from our project. There are other BAP species, such as the brown hare and West European hedgehog, on the estate too.

# A FAMILY SHOOT

Ironically I have learnt a lot more about wildlife since I started learning about the shoot, which bemuses David. He has always loved the great outdoors and shooting in equal measure. Some of his best memories are of shooting as a child with his Papa: blasting water-filled cola cans off the bridge by the lake with a rifle, aged eight; clay pigeon shooting above the lake (where he now watches our boys, Charles and Hugo, during their lessons); and then graduating to the use of a .410, for pheasants and partridge, lamping and duck flighting at Branston Ponds.

Shooting is a big part of David's life. Being surrounded by such marvellous opportunities formed the basis of his own passion and now seeing his children learn the same skills is a real thrill. He tells them a lovely tale that his father repeated many times, about the Marquess of Salisbury when he was shooting at Belvoir

*Youngsters performing at the Double Ponds drive.*

years ago. Walking to his peg, he stopped on arrival and allowed his loader to set up his shooting stick. Relieved, Lord Salisbury, a rather large gentleman, then took the weight of his feet. In a split second the stick sank deeply into the soft ground and his lordship plummeted like a stone, leaving his bottom in the mud and his feet in the air!

As for every Manners generation before us, family shoot weekends are highlights in our diaries. Preparation always starts well in advance for any shooting party to stay over, whether for family and friends or for paying guests. I run around like a hotel manager checking beds, making sure every room has fresh flowers, drinks and any essential items that may have been forgotten in the packing. Every bathroom is checked for hot water because the plumbing system is so complex that one functional bathroom can easily fool you into believing that all the hot water pipes are working.

For three weekends of the year, though, we fill the house with up to forty-five friends and family. I'm a great believer, especially now that our children are mostly in their teens, that everyone else's children should come because we want to inspire them to enjoy shooting too – and frankly it's fun all being together. In the past we've littered the floors of some very grand bedrooms with mattresses so that little ones can sleep close to their parents but, as they all get older, they spread out across the landings to be nearer their mates.

The whole event kicks off on Friday night. Our keepers meet weary travellers at the main door and dispatch luggage and take charge of the guns. We'll all meet for drinks before a casual dinner in the state dining room. This sounds very grand but actually it is a parody of a formal dinner – it is the only room big enough to seat us all together. The first night is usually a big catching-up session with friends but also an opportunity for getting to know new friends better – which works both ways of course. On one occasion, Bruce Forsyth's wife, Winnie, had come to stay with us with a girlfriend (Bruce was away, preparing for Strictly Come Dancing) and at the end of a long dinner at the table the conversation had turned to gamekeepers and ghosts. An unlikely combination, you might agree. Before everyone turned in for the night, two members of the party had sneaked out, snatched a mannequin from a corridor where it was being used to display the 9th Duke's coronation robe, and dressed it up to look like a gamekeeper. Then they left it in the half-light of

Winnie's bedroom … and you can imagine the screams when she went up to bed! She was a great sport about it though and it hasn't put her off coming to stay again.

I have never even attempted to walk the social tightrope that is etiquette, apart, that is, from common sense and politeness, so I am used to a lot of tutting, especially from my husband. One of our tenants, Bill James, plays the bagpipes and I just can't resist having him to play at 8am on the terraces to wake everyone up. We always stay up far too long on the first night of these weekends and it can be such an effort ensuring that everyone makes it to breakfast. 'Bagpipes? South of the border?' Sniff-sniff, tut-tut. Guilty as charged!

At 9am everyone congregates outside the front door to meet the loaders and to listen to any instructions from the head keeper before piling in to the Guns' bus – a converted ambulance. David's loader, Bob Baxter, loaded for him for thirty years and was a much-valued friend on any shoot, but he sadly died a couple of years ago. Now Bob's brother, Mick, has taken over. I'm afraid David doesn't operate the customary peg system where Guns are invited to draw a number for their places on each drive. He likes to shoot in the middle of the line, to the irritation of many, and so the head keeper places everyone else around him.

One of my favourite drives is Frog Hollow. It's very close to the garden and the birds erupt over the top of the trees on a steep bank. There is also a pond and it's a great place to warm up and get your eye in if duck come in.

Elevenses is at 'The Happy Beater' – the nickname for a convenient barn converted for the purpose about two miles from the castle. Mrs Horton, our housekeeper, makes the best bullshot I have ever tasted, or you can have cherry brandy, sloe gin or King's Ginger wine. We were given a very smart walnut box for picnic glasses as a wedding present, so that comes out as do hot sausages and sausage rolls. A shoot day revolves around enormous quantities of food: great if you're walking and too much if you're not.

However, after one more drive it is time for lunch back at the castle. The greatest difficulty is herding everyone in and out in time to start shooting again before tea! By the time boots have come off, shoes on, coats hung up, Guns and guests have found their way to the Guard Room for a fiery Bloody Mary prepared by our assistant, Wendy, and then warmed up in front of the blazing fires before climbing the stairs for a three-course lunch, it is time to boot and spur once more. But the shoot lunch is an integral part of a shooting day.

There are great debates as to what constitutes a perfect shoot lunch. Mostly stodgy English nursery food prevails but I'm going to name-drop and admit to making use of a recipe I was given by Elton John and David Furnish's Turkish chef that we use for a very popular starter, Moroccan lamb and couscous. It's a winner every time. Baked ham with Cumberland sauce and sticky toffee pudding to follow is rarely bettered. Before you know it, David is thumping the table to warn of a two-minute departure.

It has become a tradition to finish every family shoot with a duck and goose flight from the bridge over the lake. About eight years ago a great friend, Charlotte Hopkins, came to stay with her new husband from America, Tucker Johnson. Literally an innocent abroad, poor man, we told him that it was an ancient Belvoir tradition that whoever shot the first goose had to strip down to their boxers and retrieve it from the lake. It never occurred to any of us that this wonderful American would do so. Whether he was trying to impress his new wife or was just plain gullible we'll never know, but he did it and the memory lives long in the minds of everyone present at the time.

Duck and goose shooting starts on the first Saturday in September for family and friends and the keepers act as beaters and pickers-up. We have a lot of Canada geese that can be a problem on winter cereal crops, as well as mallard, some teal and a few other species. One has to be very quiet approaching the water so as not to spook them. A slammed car door can be ruinous and over the years I've lost count of the number of small children I've gagged and reined in as they have shrieked and slammed their way out of a Land Rover. When everyone is in place the keepers appear at the other side of the water and drive the ducks towards us. The bag is never large but watching the skill and fieldcraft of both keepers and Guns is always enjoyable.

The 9th Duke seems to have found a colossal number of ducks at the lakes during his tenure. He wrote on 20 September 1920 at 6.30pm to his cousin Captain C L Lindsay: 'Knox performed his masterstroke today – he came out shooting without his cartridges. Borrowed ten and eventually found himself on one side of the upper lake cartridgeless

with a thousand ducks coming all around him for threequarters of an hour! Wonderful!!' Needless to say the participants shot only eleven birds between them.

After our shoot, Gourmet Game Ltd from Lincolnshire collects all the game that isn't going to be used by the family or taken by the Guns. The Countryside Alliance has invested over £1.5 million over the last ten years to promote the consumption of game meat, which has seen sales increase in the UK by ninety-two per cent since the campaign started. Television chefs have also had a really positive effect on the consumer too; they are cooking lots more game than ever before.

I always try to sit in the front of the Guns' bus when I can to catch up with Big John: John Sheeron. He was the first beater I met when I came shooting with David before we were married and he made me feel so welcome. I remember asking him how long he'd been at Belvoir and he surprised me with his answer, 'twenty years underground and twenty years above'. It transpired that he had been a miner before joining the team at Belvoir as a keeper. He wears his tweed with such pride and his gold watch, awarded to him on his retirement, is always pinned to his lapel. He's a favourite with our children too and one of Violet's earliest memories is of being carried on his shoulders when she was about two-and-a-half and tired of walking.

After Mrs Horton's completely amazing coconut-honey cake and a glut of other goodies for tea, everyone retires to their rooms and meets up again in the Elizabeth Saloon for drinks before dinner. Saturday night is a black-tie event and now the children are older they all love to dress up too. After dinner our corporate shoot room becomes a disco, with karaoke and coloured lights and everyone leaves the dinner table for a dance. We did have a terrible experience with a smoke machine about three years ago. At close to three o'clock in the morning all the young were still partying and the smoke, unbeknown to anyone, had billowed its way towards a fire alarm and set off the system. Within minutes a fire engine, siren blaring, was screaming up the drive. After a totally justified rap on the knuckles for wasting their time and resources, all these burly fire personnel finished up on the dance floor for a quick bop. It was the unlikeliest end to a shoot day that I could ever have imagined and hopefully, now that the smoke machine has been binned, an unrepeatable one.

The shoot is a great way to welcome new people to Belvoir and we recently hosted a charity clay pigeon competition with Dylan Williams from the Royal Berkshire Shooting School. It was a tremendous success, raising £45,000 for Rainbows Hospice and The Willow Foundation. There were twenty-eight teams of four competing, with 200 birds offered in five simulated flushes over five drives. Apart from supporting two such deserving causes, the day provided a very worthwhile opportunity to showcase everything we have at Belvoir to a wider audience and we're hopeful of repeating such events in the future.

## THE LADIES' SHOOT

Another new departure is the ladies' shoot. My dear friend, Heather McGregor, who writes a weekly column in the *Financial Times*, loves her shooting and brought a team of girlfriends to stay with us in September 2011. She and I had first met when she came to shoot with a corporate party in 2006.

I do try to welcome as many visitors as I can personally on shoot days but with five children it isn't always easy to switch from working mum to hostess with the mostest – and on time! Back on that day in 2006 I'd been picking children up from school on a freezing cold winter's afternoon and was wrapped in a fur coat that David had bought me from a great second-hand shop in London. I may just have mentioned, even grumbled, to him once that sub-zero temperatures on a particularly cold day were penetrating the thick castle walls – and I think he thought the coat would be a good investment and cheaper than extra heating! Anyway, I was late to greet the shoot guests, so I jumped quickly out of the car, ushered the children out of the way and rushed into the Guard Hall to say hello. 'So you're the Duchess,' Heather said, smiling at me. 'Don't tell me all duchesses wear mink coats for the school run?' With that she took the contact details of the fur coat shop (subsequently buying her own) and we clicked. I love her directness and no messing attitude and I don't know anyone else who can get so much done in a day.

Heather's 2011 guests were no ordinary girls' party. The 'girls' turn out to be a serious bunch of high-achieving movers and shakers from the City, PR, law, recruitment and media firms. Heather has this amazing ability to put people together and she excelled

*Above*
*the Duchess and her girls*

*Left*
*Family and friends congregate*
*outside the castle after a*
*wonderful day.*

herself on this particular trip with twenty of her 'top team'. She is always telling me that she loves her shooting but is far too often the only woman on the line, particularly on corporate days, and wants to get more women shooting.

At the time we had a new chef cooking his first dinner, who probably hadn't expected his food to be scrutinised by twenty women – but he needn't have worried. Seasonal and local produce was all cooked well and his pudding was absolutely delicious. Amongst the guests I met Emma Weir, who runs her own financial services headhunter firm, Eban. I discovered that she has a woodcock and snipe shoot on the Isle of Muck and she invited me along to find out as much as I could for my chapter on woodcock (see Chapter 7). I sat close to Henrietta Royle, a wonderfully colourful and forthright lady, who had shot in Heather's charity clay shoot team at the Royal Berkshire Shooting School, and on the other side was a very glamorous television presenter. I was surprised how tight-knit this little group is and the big subject during dinner wasn't targets, mergers and acquisitions, but our children. The usual concerns were discussed: teenage hormones, schools and first boyfriends and girlfriends.

The next morning, a dense mist had descended, hanging thickly in the valley. It looked as if shooting could be delayed at best, cancelled at worst. But 'no' won't do, so Phil Burtt decided to escort the ladies to Frog Hollow to shoot duck, in the hope that the weather would improve later. For now the Guns would be given an opportunity to get their eye in over a relatively straightforward target. Phil had sent out for reinforcements as there were so many Guns who were novices and a team of helpers was very happy to assist. Everyone has to be a 'first timer' at some stage and Heather and Phil allocated two novices to each peg and they swapped in and out. Any squeamishness was soon dispelled by the realisation that for every duck that fell, hundreds got away. The sun broke through and it didn't take long for several shots to be fired and a few whoops of accomplishment to be heard as birds hit the ground. Everyone relaxed and I left them to it as they departed for a partridge drive. I overheard one of Phil's recruits discussing the euro with one of the Guns and I realised the chemistry of the whole party was working just as well as Heather had predicted.

By tea, several Guns had shot their first birds, the mood was electric and everyone had had a fabulous day. More to the point, as it was late September, everyone had refreshed their knowledge of the difference between a partridge and a hen pheasant!

Heather reminds me that game shooting for those who have never done it before can seem intimidating with all the requirements around safety, tipping, the draw and many other rituals. Historically many women have accompanied their menfolk to shoots but in the twenty-first century most of these career women did not have husbands who shoot, so I hope that we were able to welcome and reassure them all at Belvoir. Before the team left, they had all changed back into their business suits with briefcases and overnight bags at the ready, resuming their corporate identities after a brief, but I sincerely hope enjoyable, respite from their high-pressure lives.

I lose count of the times when I wonder what David's ancestors would make of life in their home today. But when the castle is bulging at the cornerstones with shooting parties I like to think that there would be a nod of approval that so many different people are enjoying their legacy.

*Left*
*A lady on Heather McGregor's day successfully landing her target.*

*Right*
*Our faithful 'Big John' guiding another beginner.*

# 2

# GROUSE

GROUSE SHOOTING SEASON
12 AUGUST – 10 DECEMBER

My only previous experience of grouse shooting consisted of beating on Beacon Moor above the Radnorshire village of Beguildy on my pony, Betty, with the Teme Valley Pony Club. It was an annual pilgrimage and so much fun; even my brothers who weren't keen on riding never missed it. We would power-wash the stock trailer, scrub the ponies, hook up to the Land Rover with Dad at the wheel, put a picnic in the boot and take to the hills. Health and safety rules would never allow a load of kids on ponies anywhere near guns nowadays and how lucky I am to have grown up in an era when real adventure was encouraged. Having said that, it's amazing there weren't any accidents. (We won't count the time the trailer, with three tired ponies on board, unhitched itself on the way home after a good lunch – will we, Dad?) I remember Willy, the more reckless of my brothers, kicking his pony on whilst shouting 'yee-ha', with arms and reins high in the air – not very Pony Club-like behaviour – and being rapped on the knee with a stick by the DC (District Commissioner) Ann Peters, aka 'Annie Get Your Gun'. More than a dozen of us and four or five pointers would set off to look for grouse, of which there seemed no shortage. All around us we would see wild Welsh Mountain ponies, plenty of sheep, and beautiful, beautiful country. To the Guns we must have looked like Red Indians when we appeared over the horizon but no one ever complained – I don't think.

# GLENOGIL IN THE ANGUS GLENS

I had never been on a really smart driven grouse shoot before but for my research in 2011 I was invited to accompany Phil Burtt to Glenogil, near Kirriemuir, the family home of John Dodd in the Angus Glens. There had been a lot of talk about the coming season, not least from Phil who had written about the prospects in his *Fieldsports* magazine column. Grouse shooting depends on a surplus in the breeding population and, apart from moor management, the weather is a big factor in the birds' fate. An exceptionally harsh winter had raised concerns that the grouse would have suffered but these resilient birds have proved they are great survivors. As the gamekeepers carried out their counts in July, the signs were good: expectations were high.

Arriving at Aberdeen airport in enough tweeds

to promote Scotland's entire textile industry I was given a taste of things to come by the billboard pictures there of heather moorland in the Angus Glens, carefully burned into an enchanting patchwork effect.

I had heard a lot about John Dodd and the work he has done at Glenogil. I also knew he was a co-founder of Artemis, one of the country's leading fund management companies, and that he had bought the estate in 2002. It is situated in the middle of the Angus Glens, thought by many to be the spiritual home of driven red grouse.

We arrived late, in the dark, but in time for a delicious dinner with the rest of the house party. During coffee in the drawing-room I caught up with John. He is very easy to talk to and dressed in jeans, t-shirt and a fabulous diamond earring, an appearance not dissimilar to that of an old-style rock star, makes for a refreshingly modern-day laird. But why buy a shoot, and why in Scotland? Surely he could have bought uncomplicated luxury anywhere in the world? Quite simply it appears Glenogil offered a chance to experience the beating heart of a stunning grouse moor and the endless diversity that comes with this sporting estate. John learnt to shoot as a young adult and has lost none of his youthful energy – a very necessary requirement as I am finding out.

There is nothing obviously flash about this estate but you are left in no doubt that huge sums of money are needed to underpin the idyll. John seems to be a master of discretion but he has made his money in the City and makes no secret of the fact that his chosen lifestyle isn't cheap. Glenogil is much more than a swanky home; he has bought into a commitment to this corner of the Angus Glens. He has created a significant number of extra jobs, brought in holiday makers to stay in rental properties on the estate and his own visitors no doubt all contribute to ringing tills when they stop at shops, filling stations and pubs. But the expenditure is continuous; apart from extensive work on the moor, he has renovated all the estate houses as well as two bothies, a couple of lodges, a greenhouse and a walled garden. That's before you start on estate maintenance and building over thirty miles of road networks, nine miles of fencing to keep deer out, over 300 concrete water troughs on the dry moors and thirty new lines of butts. This is a place that needs deep pockets but more than that, someone who really believes in it.

The morning kicked off with a full English breakfast. Guns were asked to congregate outside the front door at 9am to meet their loaders, keepers and the young

head keeper, Danny Lawson, all of whom were dressed in immaculate tweeds. The pattern had been specially created for Lord Forres for his staff to wear when he owned the estate before the First World War. John's children are joining us but aren't old enough to shoot yet and, as John emphasised, 'they will need to learn to beat before they join a line of Guns'. That is a sentiment which I applaud, despite my own children having been a bit spoilt at home – though it has always been drummed into them that respect for the quarry is of paramount importance.

Standing in the first butt of the morning on the Shepherd Hill Drive, soaking up the atmosphere of this utterly magical scene, my dreamy thoughts are interrupted rather abruptly. On top of the hill behind us an elderly gentleman is purposefully lowering his tweeds, his large pale derrière exposed for all to see, and without further ado, he relieves himself. Shortly afterwards he corrected his déshabillé and returned to his butt, no doubt feeling much lighter for the experience. No one batted an eyelid. Some of our American clients would have had a fit of the vapours if they had seen that at Belvoir. 'You British!' they always say when someone behaves even remotely unconventionally.

But back to the grouse: our butt saw plenty of action. Phil Burtt doesn't appear to do anything else at this time of year except lighten the skies and moors with his share of grouse, taking no prisoners.

We talked about heather, which covers seventy-five per cent of the 20,000-acre estate, across three glens, Glenogil, Glen Moy and Glenquiech, as well as the Fern and Nathro beats, and how it requires precision management. The patchwork effect in the pictures I saw at Aberdeen airport, like here, is the result of regular burning. This keeps the heather young and healthy, as it is forced to produce new shoots. If left alone the plants grow long and rank.

By law, burning has to be done between 1 October and 10 April (15 April in England). The best time to do it is when the peat is wet and the wind is light but it's a great skill to keep the fire under full control. If it burns too strongly it will not only damage the roots of the plants but also catch alight the underlying peat, destroying seeds and causing erosion. You can cut heather with a mower too but it's an expensive and difficult process over rocks and uneven ground. The wonderful shades of colour you can see in the patchwork clearly illustrate the cycle of burning.

Heather beetle has wiped out one drive this year. As grubs these insects wreak devastation on very young and very old heather plants, munching their way through shoots and stems, turning them rusty red. In good years, small parasitic wasps deposit their eggs into the beetle larvae which eventually kills them but a warm early spring can result in greater numbers of beetle to wasp and the natural cycle is broken, leaving the heather under attack. For Danny the keeper, it's a worry for both this season and next, as big stocks of grouse will suffer and he'll have to burn the heather off and start all over again before the drive will be back in production.

As the hooter blows after the second drive everyone retrieves their birds and we pick only the ones I have marked on the butt card to make the job easier.

Walking back to the 4x4 I met a young Gun called Wenty Beaumont and his devoted loader, Tommy Dobson. Tommy loaded for Wenty's father and has known young Wenty all his life. He taught him and other members of his family to shoot and loading for him now is clearly a joy for both parties. From where I was standing his education had been thorough so I asked Tommy if his protégé had any bad habits. Without hesitation, the lovely old pro replied, 'Aye, he won't stand still!' But he added quickly, with a big smile, 'seriously though, he fidgets, but he's a very good shot'.

During my day I also learnt more about the entire grouse family. The black grouse or blackcock, slightly larger than the red grouse, is rare, due largely to changes in land use and habitat loss. These birds like to roam on moorland managed for red grouse, benefiting from the associated predator control, and close to woodland or forest-edge habitats. They are not protected but most shoots discourage you from shooting them and you'll probably be fined if you do. On the whole they are confined to Scotland and the North Pennines, though there are a few hundred in Wales too. The male, with his glossy blue-black plumage, striking red wattles, white wing bars and lyre-shaped tail is easy to identify, especially during the courtship ritual known as lekking. The greyhen is greyish-brown and smaller than her male counterpart.

Capercaillie, weighing roughly nine pounds, is the largest and rarest species in the UK's grouse family, and protected. There are less than a thousand birds left and they live exclusively in Scottish conifer

*Above*
*Charles retrieving his first grouse*

woodland, feeding on pine needles and young shoots. The species became extinct in Scotland, Ireland and northern England in the eighteenth century but were reintroduced into Scotland for shooting purposes in the mid-1800s. The male is similar in appearance to the blackcock, with a red wattle, but is larger and has no white wing bars. He can get quite aggressive during lekking. The female, although a little larger than the greyhen, again looks similar with its fairly dullcoloured plumage.

Finally, there is the ptarmigan: the smallest but toughest and most resilient of all the grouse family. Mostly living above the snow line at 3,000 feet (900m) or more, they have an ingenious moulting pattern that leaves them pure white in the winter and speckled in summer, for optimum camouflage as the remote and rocky landscape changes with the seasons. Shooting these birds is for hardy enthusiasts but a remarkable experience by all accounts for the sheer feat of finding them across such difficult terrain.

On the way to the next drive, I bumped into a London art dealer I hadn't seen for years. We were in full flow catching up when I noticed a Gun in a nearby butt signalling me over towards him in an agitated manner. 'For God's sake, be quiet,' he hissed, 'you're meant to be silent approaching a grouse butt.'

Sitting next to John Dodd at lunchtime, enjoying another gourmet feast, I tell him about the buzzard and kestrel I've seen circling above on our way to the bothy. John is proud of all the wildlife that has increased in the eight or so years that he's been here but he has had his share of problems. In 2006 Glenogil was at the centre of an unprecedented raid from up to an astonishing sixty police officers from several forces who, after an apparent tip-off from Scottish Executive and RSPB officials, flooded the estate with personnel in search of illegal poisons believed to be the cause of 'wildlife crime'. The head keeper was handcuffed and arrested and remanded in custody despite a complete lack of evidence. Incredibly the case rumbled on. John, and his staff, strongly denied any wrongdoing, no one was charged and no one has ever appeared in court – and yet his farming subsidy was cut by £107,000 as a direct result of the claims made against his estate. Allegations continue but to no avail and no charges have ever been brought. I mention all this because it is a well-documented situation and I find it so hard to accept that a man as conscientious as John, who runs

his estate with such integrity, can be the target of such seemingly malicious injustice.

The enormous road network that he has built for easier access to the moors has opened the estate to walking groups and bird-watchers and they are all very welcome. Emergency and rescue services have benefited too. A walker and a young man on a quad bike were each involved in separate accidents recently and were able to receive treatment from paramedics a lot sooner than they would have done before.

On my left at lunch was seated another friend of John's, Harry Ansell, a very funny man who made me hoot with laughter as he described his obsession with eating grouse – for breakfast, lunch and dinner. He likes them lightly roasted, for about eighteen minutes, with a knob of butter and a sprinkling of salt and pepper.

I was interested to note that none of the Guns drank alcohol at lunch. Some shoots discourage drinking as a safety precaution but I dare say no one needs extra stimulation on this shoot anyway.

After another couple of thrilling drives, Danny Lawson sounded his hooter to signal the end of a fascinating and informative day on my first driven grouse shoot. I left with such a buzz that any thoughts of tiredness were swept away as I drove home. I realised how addictive this sport could become and I didn't even shoot! Scottish moors have a compelling and bewitching wildness to them which draws you in and I can see how easy it would be to stay indefinitely.

I bumped into Robbie Douglas Miller recently, and was fascinated to hear about a new initiative he is chairing: the Wildlife Estates Scotland (WES)[1]. Robbie, the former managing director of Jenners (his family's Edinburgh department store, until it was sold in 2005) bought the 3,000-acre estate of Horseupcleugh in the heart of the Lammermuir Hills five years ago. He has always been very enthusiastic about shooting and this was an opportunity to develop his own commercially viable grouse moor. He didn't waste any time in making the necessary changes: cutting back on sheep, selling his cows and improving the heather for red grouse. As well as working on his moor at home he was chairman of the Scottish GWCT for four years until 2009 and was ready to take on another challenge. WES was launched in November 2010 to encourage Scottish landowners to 'answer the call' of wildlife and sign up to the industry-led quality assurance scheme that demonstrates how effective biodiversity is managed by Scotland's rural and sporting estate landowners. In other words how land management practices benefit biodiversity and wildlife habitats, which can ultimately stimulate the rural economy. They already have the support of over 200 farms and estates and I have no doubt that that number will increase very quickly.

[1] For more information see website: www.scottishlandandestates. co.uk and click on Wildlife Estates Scotland on the side bar.

## BEACON MOOR IN THE RADNORSHIRE HILLS

Fired up by my visit to Glenogil, I was curious to know what had become of the Beacon shoot in the Radnorshire hills. The family of Ann Price and her brother, Peter Hood, had rented the 5,000-acre grouse moor from the Crown Estate since 1948. Even though we had lost touch I was longing to see if or how the shoot had changed. To my delight Ann and Peter were still around and happy to see me.

Phil Burtt came with me as he is always interested in any grouse moor, especially one that he doesn't know. Once Ann and Peter and I had caught up with each other's news, we broached the subject of the Beacon shoot. Sadly, as is the case with many Welsh moors, grouse have almost disappeared from it in the last thirty-five years and only one had been shot there since 2009. The family still celebrate the Glorious Twelfth with their syndicate and a picnic, like the old days – only without an unwieldy gang of Pony Club children. Having shot eight days a year in the 1970s they now venture out only twice. They still maintain the land as best they can but finances are stretched. Peter, worried after two years without a sighting, resorted to putting partridges down to keep his syndicate happy. Beaters are still on horseback and on the two days out in 2011, a few more grouse were seen: an encouraging sign.

Identifying exactly what has gone wrong is difficult as, like many problems, there is a plethora of possible causes. Figures from the GWCT estimate that the number of grouse shot every year in Wales between 1911 and 1980 has fallen by eighty-two per cent with a particularly steep fall from the mid-1970s onwards: unfortunately counts are almost negligible today.

On the Beacon there is a constant battle to balance the progress of farming methods with their effects on wildlife. Between 1950 and the 1970s up to thirty brace of grouse were being shot annually, but since then new farming methods have both helped and hindered the grouse population. A marked increase in the number of sheep became a factor, because amongst other things the injection used to control fluke and scab was systemic which, in turn, killed the dung beetle and other insects that the grouse chicks fed on. Now most sheep are dipped and their numbers have dropped considerably allowing a better habitat for the grouse. In the 1960s farmers were paid to drain the surrounding farmland, which Peter believes dried up the moor and thus essential drinking water: again an important source of insect food for chicks was lost. Radnorshire Wildlife Trust has since paid for ponds to be built, restoring the supply. But that's not all. After the serious outbreak of foot-and-mouth in 2001 you were no longer allowed to leave dead stock on the hill. Unfortunately for grouse, sparrow hawks, buzzards and kites have been protected by law since 1954 and numbers have increased enormously in the last fifteen years. They eat meat and Peter is sure these carrion species are eating live chicks instead of stripping carcasses. It is perhaps no coincidence either that curlews, plovers, larks and songbirds have diminished in numbers. And then there are modern-day predators: joyriders and offroaders who rip through the moor and destroy nesting and breeding habitats. And so it goes on. There doesn't appear to be enough cohesion between landowners, the Welsh Assembly and shooting associations to try to emulate the progress made in the north of England and Scotland or indeed, and perhaps more pertinently, there is a distinct lack of deep-pocketed investors. Maybe Wales just isn't fashionable enough. Ann's son will one day take over but Beacon will be a very different moor to the one we knew as children.

We left Peter and Ann and walked back up the moor, I with sentimental memories of my childhood in the 1970s. I know it was never a grand, professionally keepered concern but countless hard-working, passionate custodians have devoted a lot of time, money and effort over the years to securing their sport. As I looked around I could see that bracken has taken a strong hold in many places and more heather needs burning off. Much forestry has been planted too since I last visited and I find it so frustrating that such a prime example of a Welsh grouse moor may forever be confined to memory with so little chance of it returning in reality.

But good news: when I got home I read in the GWCT's magazine that talks between the GWCT, fifty moor owners and managers in Wales and the Countryside Council for Wales (CCW) have started to find out how grouse management could be achieved within current Welsh agri-environment schemes and complement wider conservation objectives. How wonderful it would be to see grouse return to Beacon.

# THE HOWDEN AND DERWENT MOORS

On the way home, Phil told me about an incredible man, Geoff Eyres, who has restored 6,500 acres of National Trust-owned moorland in Derbyshire to a superb wildlife, and grouse, habitat.

A week later we visited him at his farm in Brough. Nothing could have prepared me for Geoff's impassioned and dedicated determination. When he took on the sporting lease of the Howden and Derwent moors in the Peak District in 1989, he counted only six wild birds on the vast but species-poor grassland areas. Heath species were missing and despite a supportive programme from the Environmentally Sensitive Areas (ESA) scheme, not much was changing for the better. Heather seed does not germinate easily but as a trained agronomist and having also worked for a scientific plant breeding company, he wondered whether he could artificially induce it to do so by smoke. He had read about studies in South Africa in 1993 that suggested fire could stimulate germination. He also noticed midge larvae eating germinated seeds in young heather flowers but where heather had been burnt, this inhibited the larvae hatch for that year and it grew back much better. After several failed attempts Geoff developed a winning system that combined treated seed with controlled grass burning.

The next problem was how to sow heather seed on a large scale on difficult terrain. By good fortune, Geoff is also a keen machinery enthusiast and in typical style he designed and built appropriate equipment that could tackle the contours. Areas completely beyond reach were sown from a helicopter. Geoff doesn't give up easily.

His success has been enormous, restoring thousands of acres of barren moorland to thriving, heather-rich grouse moor. Skylarks, pipits, golden plover, curlew, ring-ouzel, snipe, short-eared owls, white hares, dunlin and lapwings are all on the increase and black game has been regularly sighted, as have peregrines, merlins, buzzards and even ravens along with the more familiar goshawks. Recent surveys have shown that Howden moor is a jewel in the crown of moorland wildlife.

The grouse numbers are healthy enough to provide the shooting syndicate with eight days' sport, which have seen 800 brace shot in a season. What is more, the project has been mostly self-financed. Geoff has done most of the work himself with a keeper, spending thousands of machine hours a year seed-collecting, spraying, burning, applying seed and following up. He has dedicated twenty obsessional years to improving the bracken and grass species to provide wildlife heath havens. He has worked early mornings, late evenings and most weekends and covered the majority of the seven-figure cost himself, with only a little help from his landlords, The National Trust, for some fencing. Not surprisingly, the Howden Regeneration Project has won many awards, including first prize in the 2005 Purdey Awards for Game Conservation.

I left in awe. Here is a man who has almost single-handedly transformed five moors, with ambitions to restore many more. He has increased the bio-diversity, added to the local economy with his shoot and has probably done more to increase wildlife in the Pennines than anyone else in living memory. So I was horrified when Phil told me that Geoff's keeper, Glenn Brown, was convicted in 2011 for misusing a crow pen to trap a bird of prey. An undercover RSPB investigator had filmed just seven seconds of Glenn visiting the pen. It was claimed that it was being misused (these traps are legally used to catch crows, rooks and jackdaws) and that a dead sparrowhawk was found in a bush thirty metres from the trap. These accusations led to Glenn's prosecution and conviction. For the record, he vehemently denies the charges and his case is subject to an appeal.

As an outsider, I can't help thinking how much more we have to lose if we don't work together with the RSPB and other associations to target the real issues in our countryside: to preserve and manage all wildlife for everyone. Surely, allowing for controlled culling of excessive raptor populations, which would protect very many more vulnerable species in the food chain, makes more sense.

# THE LANGHOLM MOOR PROJECT

An initiative that is examining whether a concerted approach can sustain a modern shoot is the Langholm Moor Demonstration Project on the Duke of Buccleuch's estate in Dumfriesshire. I talked to Dr Adam Smith, chair of the project's public relations committee, to find out more.

The project has been set up to assess whether traditional moorland management and novel techniques, such as diversionary feeding, can allow a hen harrier

*Above*
*No heather shortage on*
*Geoff Eyre's moorland above*
*Lady Bower reservoir in the*
*Peak District.*

*Langholm Moor on the Duke of Buccleuch's estate in Dumfriesshire.*

*Left*
*Two of our children, Alice and*
*Hugo, leading the way on their*
*first walked-up grouse day at*
*Westerdale in North Yorkshire.*

population in good conservation status to co-exist with a grouse moor.

It all started in 2007, after two years of planning, when Michael Russell, the Scottish Minister for Environment, launched the most ambitious land management and conservation project of its kind. It is a unique partnership between Buccleuch Estates, Scottish Natural Heritage (SNH), the GWCT, RSPB and Natural England, which could ultimately end up investing £3million over a ten-year period in moorland management and in employment. In order to deliver the project's multiple objectives there is a part-time team: a project manager, researchers and a seasonal student, with a full-time scientist and five keepers led by Simon Lester, former head keeper at Belvoir and Holkham in Norfolk. As well as trying to find a middle ground between raptor and grouse management, this highly experienced team hopes to re-establish a driven grouse shoot on Langholm Moor that will support moorland management, increase bio-diversity and benefit the rural economy.

So why is this project needed? Back in the early twentieth century this roughly 7,600-hectare upland moor was a hugely successful grouse shoot. The number of grouse shot declined from 1948, not primarily because of raptor predation but because the area of heather moor shrank by forty-eight per cent. However even this loss left a fine driven moor with occasional bags of over 2,000 brace from the 1970s to 1990s. The 'occasional' big bags were because, in common with most other moors of the time, parasitic worm burdens caused grouse numbers to suffer a cycle of peaks and troughs every six or seven years. However, from 1992 to 1996, the first Langholm Project, or Joint Raptor Study, followed a new trend in the grouse population; the cycle stopped and grouse numbers declined to very low levels. This suppression of the normal cycle was not worm- or habitat-driven but the result of raptor predation, notably by peregrine falcons over winter and by hen harriers on grouse broods in the summer. Without any grouse or ability to control this predation pressure the Buccleuch Estates would not keeper the moor and from 1999 to 2007 it was pretty much left to its own devices except for sheep grazing.

But the monitoring of numbers of raptors, grouse and other birds of interest such as crows and waders which started in 1992 continued, tracking the

*Opposite page*
*George Padley with Charles Manners on his first*
*walked-up grouse day*

*Below*
*Grouse approaching the line.*

further steady decline in grouse and lapwing numbers and the rise of the crows. This depressing trend was slightly mitigated when, between 1998 and 1999, a research trial was set up to feed nesting hen harriers with day-old poultry chicks and dead white rats, the intention being to divert the harriers from feeding on grouse broods – hence 'diversionary feeding'. The results were interesting, as no grouse chicks were reported being brought back to the carefully monitored harrier nests. But for all the optimism, however, there was no measurable increase in the grouse stock. At the same time, the number of hen harriers collapsed and all parties realised they had lost out.

That is where the new project came in; a balanced recovery of both grouse and harriers was needed. Legal predator control of foxes, crows, stoats and weasels, disease control for grouse, as well as the diversionary feeding techniques are all essential if there is any chance of meeting the project's objectives. A very significant part of the current project is to improve and extend the heather moorland habitat for all moorland breeding birds through burning, bracken control and appropriate stock management. In this way grouse chicks may avoid the claws of the hen harriers by finding plenty of food and cover amongst the young heather shoots, while waders and hen harriers will have somewhere to nest.

So how's it going? The independent experts who make up the project's Science and Technical Advisory Group (STAG) review the project's progress every three years for viability. Just last year, in 2011, they felt that the project should continue to meet its targets. Progress has been made on habitat management and the innovative work being done to overcome the difficulties of recovering the heather – not helped by the destructive effects of heather beetle – is beginning to show. But there are still too few grouse to shoot this year while harrier and wader numbers don't appear to have responded to the improved management. Understanding what is driving these populations – be it weather, food supply or predation by species which cannot currently be legally controlled, such as buzzards – will be critical in future years so that management of the moor can be further fine-tuned.

Everyone with an interest in grouse shooting is watching to see how the project develops. Simon Lester tells me: 'It is already demonstrating how organisations can work together for the good of the

*Above*
*George Padley guiding Charles to shoot his first grouse.*

*Right*
*End of a successful day at Westerdale.*
*Left to right, shoot manager, Jim Chatterway, Alice Manners,*
*Eliza Manners, Emma Rutland, Hugo Manners,*
*Charles Granby and keeper, Jimmy Brough.*

uplands. Cooperation and understanding will be vital in securing a future for shooting and wildlife management.' If the project succeeds, it will provide invaluable information for all those who seek modern sustainable grouse management across the UK.

Good shooting brings people to otherwise isolated areas and boosts local economies. In Scotland, according to figures from the GWCT, grouse shooting generates £23.3million per annum and provides more than 1000 full-time jobs. Figures from the Moorland Association[2] reported in excess of £67.7million spent on grouse shooting in England and Wales last year. Moor owners spent £52.5million of that figure managing their estates.

On the moors that we have visited it is easy to see where the money goes and statistics are further evidence that grouse shooting benefits the environment: a controversial point in the media. Over the last ten years grouse-moor managers in England have paid for heather to be brought back to 89 square miles of moorlands, and plugged miles of moorland drainage ditches to lock up carbon in the peaty soil, with a further 823 miles planned; sown heather seed over 26 square miles; improved or built 257 miles of traditional dry stone walls and fencing to help manage sheep grazing; treated 65 square miles of invasive bracken to stop it swamping and killing other moorland plants; created 4,485 mini moorland ponds which benefit insects, water vole and amphibians; planted over 1.1million native trees in moorland gills, recreating lost habitat, especially for the rare black grouse; and employed twenty-five per cent more gamekeepers to manage the moorland.

# WESTERDALE IN NORTH YORKSHIRE

My last outing to a prime grouse moor was on the 4,500-hectare estate at Westerdale in North Yorkshire. Phil Burtt had been instrumental in its purchase in 2008 for his friend David Ross, of Carphone Warehouse fame, and subsequently advised him about moor management. After a slow start due to teething problems the moor is once more producing record bags.

David had very kindly invited us all for a halfday walked-up grouse shoot in early September 2011. With only a few days to go before my youngest child, Hugo, left the nest for prep school it was a perfect opportunity to

keep everyone busy and focused. Sadly eighteen-year-old Violet, our eldest child, and my husband, David, couldn't be with us so the boys and I, Phil, his assistant George Padley and Oliver Fountain on work experience all travelled north in convoy. En route we picked up the other girls, Alice, then sixteen, and Eliza, fourteen, from their school in Yorkshire, to join their brothers Charles, eleven, and Hugo, eight, in the car.

We arrived at the lodge and quickly changed into jeans and boots and made our way to the shoot lodge to eat our picnic lunch. Alice was already complaining that she didn't like walking. David Ross was about to have lunch with his team of friends and graciously invited us all to join him. Who should I bump into at the table but my new best friend, the obsessive grouse eater, Harry Ansell! I can only think that there are a lot of empty desks at this time of year. After another hearty and enjoyable lunch sans alcohol we take our separate ways. David and his friends head off to the butts whilst our party set off, with assorted dogs, to walk the moor. Phil tells us that the grouse fly a little bit slower across Yorkshire's undulating landscape than they do in Scotland and so should be a little bit easier for novices to shoot. But we're here for the experience and if anyone shoots anything it will be a bonus!

Hugo's wellies are too big making him stumble in the heather and Alice still grumbles with each stride. Then, without warning, a covey of grouse appears from nowhere and takes us all by surprise. Charles pulls his trigger and to everyone's astonishment he hits his target and grounds his first grouse. Alice isn't far behind and suddenly fires her gun, bagging her first grouse too. The triumphant but hushed excitement between them is so tangible I want to bottle it. They shoot another two birds each: Alice now strides out with purpose. Eliza and I are not so lucky – sometimes birds fly towards you and sometimes they don't. Similarly, sometimes you can hit everything that moves and other times you can't seem to aim straight when the bird is staring down your barrels.

We finished the afternoon with four very happy children, two of whom had shot their very first grouse: it was a huge honour to be given the opportunity and an experience they will never forget. Hugo, too young to shoot, had loved being on the moor watching the grouse and the dogs' skills. I noticed he had slunk off with Phil shortly after we had finished but at the time

[2] See website: www.moorlandassociation.org

thought no more about it.

We made our way back to the house. David and his party arrived back soon after and we were all treated to a huge and very jolly tea. The boys were catching up with the cricket score on an enormous flat-screen television and we were all tucking in to lashings of sandwiches and cake when suddenly the door burst open and Hugo shouts 'Yes!' He stood triumphant in the doorway, blood on his beaming face from his 'blooding', with a dead grouse in each hand! Phil had taken him out with a .410 and Hugo had shot not one but two grouse, not only keeping up with his siblings but I suspect also establishing a thirst for this sport of kings that I hope will stay with him for ever. I only wish Violet and my husband David could have been with us too.

*Below The all-important shoot lunch.*

# WEMMERGILL

Over the last few years some moors have seen grouse proliferate beyond anyone's wildest dreams. Medicated grit and eye-watering sums of personal investment are undoubtedly the main reasons for this. But what of the future? Grouse are notorious for flirting with near extinction from disease and adverse weather conditions, so I rang Michael Cannon, owner of Wemmergill – one of the finest grouse moors in the country – to ask him what kind of future he sees for grouse shooting.

'I see the next few years as being incredibly exciting. At no previous time in the history of driven grouse shooting has there been such a combination of new ownership, new ideas, new investment, and new technology. Looking at the two greatest years in Wemmergill's history: 1872 (8,532 brace) happened soon after driven grouse shooting became widespread in the 1860s and before there was any real understanding of grouse behaviour. And in 1934 (8,459 brace) Sir Ian Walker was lucky enough to start his tenancy at a time when a huge stock must have been left the previous year that disease had luckily not wiped out. It wasn't a great season breeding-wise, as the young to old ratio was only two to one, so there must have just been a phenomenal number of pairs left. We are now much more scientific about counting birds in the spring and in July; more aware of the need for medicated grit to counter the dreaded strongyle worm and really much more professional about running our moors than ever they were in the past.

'As long as non-shooting officialdom leaves us to get on with maintaining these wonderful tracts of wild land in a way that continues to benefit them, as it has done in the past, then the immediate future for the red grouse looks wonderful. As has often been said in the past, our wild game birds are in no danger of extinction from those who shoot them, but under severe threat from those who simply don't understand – or don't want to understand – the benefits to all wildlife from what we are doing.'

Michael Cannon's achievements seem even more remarkable when you consider that he had never picked up a gun until 1987 when he was fifty-seven. No one should ever think they are too old to learn to shoot. Bitten by the bug, he has since spent an astronomical £20million buying and then improving Wemmergill.

Wemmergill is arguably the most coveted of all grouse moors; its beguiling natural beauty coupled with its phenomenal shooting success and history is an astonishing possession. For nearly 450 years it had been the playground for the late Queen Mother's family, the Bowes Lyons. Practically every leading sporting alpha male has graced the game books. One particularly impressive entry that stands out was when Sir Frederick Milbank was reported to have killed 190 grouse in 25 minutes during his tenancy in the great grouse year of 1872. English royalty, The Kaiser, Emperor Wilhelm who was honoured with a butt named after him, MPs, novelists, pop stars and footballers have all contributed to the long roll-call of notables, celebrities and other legendary tenants, who include Sir Joseph Nickerson and Sir Tom Cowie.

This is a grouse moor where it has never been unusual to bag vast numbers of birds. Examples from the records for 1872 and 1934 are mentioned above but an annual average of 1,871 brace between 1902 and 2002 gives perspective to the current annual average for the last five years: 7,778 brace! In 2009 a new record was established, with 8,645 brace.

Mr Cannon senior was in the RAF during the Second World War, and was away most of the time. Michael's uncle was stationed in India and – like everyone – the rest of the family at home had to endure rationing, often to the point of near-starvation. Occasional food parcels stuffed with exotic dried fruits, sent from India by his uncle, were a huge treat. Despite the war Michael's business acumen was developing and he quickly learnt to earn some money selling white mice to his classmates, his first venture. His entrepreneurial spirit led to fortunes being made from the poultry and brewing industries and it was only when he bought into the Devenish Brewery that he had his first taste of shooting. Corporate days were already booked in the diary and seeing the obvious networking potential, he felt obliged to attend as an onlooker.

His own first shooting day took place a year later. Armed with a Browning 12-bore, he went to Abbotsbury on the Fleet in Dorset, with seven fellow Guns. The whole day provided a vivid memory. It started with a breakfast of porridge sprinkled with demerara sugar, loosened with a splash of Drambuie, and ended with a total of 267 pheasants, of which he could account for about 26. It was a tremendous start to what was to become a lifetime's future commitment. He

*Opposite page*
*David Kerr with Peter Greening (left)*
*at Glenogil.*

*Transporting Guns and beaters across rough terrain on a grouse moor isn't easy but these caterpillar wheels make light work of towing the Guns' bus at Glenogil.*

# PHIL BURTT'S TOP TIPS FOR GROUSE SHOOTING

**Double guns** – In most cases grouse are shot with double guns but if you are inexperienced or you are not happy, my advice would always be to shoot with one gun. Double guns only enable you to have more than two shots in one covey. Experienced shots need to remember to shoot birds well out in front because if you only manage to shoot one gun into a covey the chances are you have left it too late to use the second.

**Butt frames** – Always use butt frames – a three-sided framework on the side of the butt, supplied on nearly all grouse moors – to stop your swing before your barrels reach your neighbour. It also prevents you starting your swing too soon (while in line with the gun) when the bird has gone through the line and you shoot behind.

**Start of the drive** – There might not always be a hooter to signal the beginning of a drive, so be prepared.

**Poaching others' birds** – Unlike any other quarry you are free to shoot any grouse that is either crossing the butt or your neighbour's butt. If it is in your arc you can shoot it. Poaching is more acceptable on grouse moors.

**Concentrate** – Concentration is of paramount importance at all times more than for any other quarry. Grouse can appear from low-lying dips, at any angle and at times from behind.

**Be quiet** – Keep talking to a minimum and keep it quiet.

**Beaters and flankers** – Remember the beaters. There could be as many as six of them walking towards you. If you feel they are too close and you haven't heard the hooter to stop you shooting in front, do not shoot. If you are in butt 1 and 2 or 8 and 9 you need to be aware of the flankers too. They are always in range of birds crossing wide of the Guns so always make a mental note of where they are. And, very importantly, say good morning and have a chat; they will be walking miles to put grouse up towards you and we all like to feel appreciated.

**Hooter** – The head keeper will talk you through the safety aspects before you start and explain what the various blasts on a hooter will signal. But basically you will hear one when the beaters approach, to signal that you can only shoot behind, and the final hooter at the end of a drive is a signal to stop shooting and put your gun back in its sleeve and start picking up.

**What to wear** – Grouse can see! You need to be well camouflaged. I once saw a beautiful blonde girl being reprimanded by the head keeper for not wearing a hat because her wonderful hair might divert the grouse. Also, because the weather in August can be so changeable, remember to keep waterproofs close by in case of heavy rain.

**Midges** – Be prepared for midges. When the wind drops they can be quite unbearable, so take appropriate repellents.

**Tipping** – The owner of the moor or the agent running the day will normally advise on tipping.

**Dogs** – Dogs are always welcome on grouse moors but please make sure that unruly ones are always kept well tethered.

**Butt companions** – A butt companion needs to be out of the Gun's way, wearing ear defenders and ready to mark the butt card as your birds fall, to speed retrieving at the end of the drive. Also remember that Guns, particularly if he or she has their own dog, like to pick up their own birds so be as careful as possible to mark your quarry. It is a cardinal sin to pick someone else's birds.

**Footpaths** – Grouse moors are covered with public footpaths. At all times you must remain vigilant for anyone else on the moors, especially behind you.

---

was fortunate too that his beloved wife, Sally, to whom he has been married for forty-four years, was as keen on the sport as he was. They learnt to shoot together in a disused quarry at the back of their house in Dorset and by all accounts they are as good as each other. 'She took to it like a duck to water,' says Michael proudly.

They subsequently started their own shoot at home. Our head keeper at Belvoir, Tim Rolfe, was head keeper for the Cannons for six years and speaks very fondly of his times with them. I can detect a wistful tone when he talks about his experiences there in their early years; a shared learning journey is difficult to beat and hard to leave.

These days the Cannons spend four months a year at Wemmergill. The record bags, the glory and the splendour make good reading but the devil is never far from the heels of its riches. Few moors it seems have avoided tabloid headlines for one reason or another. The *Daily Mail* reported in January 2008, 'Multi-millionaire ruined a £5million estate that was in Queen Mother's family for generations'. How? Well, cutting to the chase: Natural England had objected to allegedly new tracks and car parking areas, resulting in a prolonged and costly court case. It is to me quite unfathomable how any organisation associated with the improvement of private land and property through private means for the benefit of wildlife, the local community and our heritage, can sometimes overlook the bigger picture. Without necessary infrastructure, progress will be limited. Michael sounds quite sanguine about the matter but says carefully, 'There are people within [these organisations] who are perverting the course of justice for their own interests.' He adds, 'There needs to be balance in our countryside. People who live and work in our rural communities have the most vested interests in how they are run and should be allowed to manage them.'

Thankfully, no amount of trouble can steal the real headlines of this story: an eighty per cent increase in all wildlife on Wemmergill moor in the last ten years; £2million spent on gamekeepers' houses and buildings; £3million spent on infrastructure, fencing, heather burning; £300,000 spent on the annual staff bill and £750,000 pumped into the local economy every season. As a result of Michael Cannon's investment, this local area has matured into a thriving rural community – and all because of his love of grouse shooting. How much has changed since my first day on a Shropshire grouse moor in the 1970s: a serious decline in the number of red grouse on most moors in Wales, a significant increase in raptors and predators across the UK, and a growing bureaucracy seemingly everywhere. On the plus side, improved management and enormous investment from arguably the new industrial scions of our age has given many English and some Scottish moors a flavour of their former glory in the great Victorian and Edwardian eras.

# 3
# GREY PARTRIDGE & WILD BIRDS

PARTRIDGE SHOOTING SEASON
1 SEPTEMBER – 1 FEBRUARY

*Grey partridge, Perdix perdix,
also known as the Englishman
and the subject of many
conservation projects across
the country.*

I have to confess that when I started to research this chapter I had a fair knowledge of our commercial red leg partridge but knew very little about greys. David had occasionally and rather excitedly pointed them out to me but I had never asked why they were so amazing. In fact I'm ashamed to admit it now, but I couldn't differentiate with total confidence between the common red leg, or Frenchman, and a native grey, this king of lowland game birds, the Englishman.

By coincidence, we had just received an invitation to a talk by the Duke of Northumberland about his grey partridge project at Alnwick but I didn't want to accept without knowing something about this special bird first. I had to learn fast and I have to thank David, Phil Burtt and Mike Barnes, his editor at *Fieldsports* magazine, for bringing me up to speed in time for our trip to Christie's King Street sale-room in London to listen to Ralph Northumberland's presentation.

I learnt how these plump, orange-faced little birds are in rapid decline because they have been affected by the changes in our environment more than any other game species. Partridge shooting in England today is very different from how it was thirty to forty years ago when there was still an abundance of wild greys. Even up until the mid-1970s it was not unusual in places like Norfolk and parts of Lincolnshire to expect bags of over a hundred brace. There were plenty of them on the edges of grouse moors in England and Scotland too. The last big years proved to be the long hot summers of 1975 and 1976. Nobody, by all accounts, would have predicted the extent to which numbers would fall: the decline was so dramatic. Figures released in 2011 show that eighty-six per cent have been lost across the country since then. Why? The answer appears to be a combination of factors – intensive farming, commercial shooting and heavy predation.

Fortunately, during the last ten years rescue plans have been initiated. The Game and Wildlife Conservation Trust (GWCT) – appointed the lead partner in 1998 under a government BAP scheme – set up the Grey Partridge Recovery Project in 2002 on a collection of seven separate farms, covering 2,500 acres near Royston in Hertfordshire. This incredible organisation implemented its own vast research programme and enjoyed some extraordinary results. The gamekeeper, Malcolm Brockless, who restored wild pheasants to a Leicestershire farm at Loddington

(the Allerton Project), started with a handful of greys and built the stock in six years to 876, with similar numbers of wild red legs and pheasants. Within five years a bag of over 100 brace of wild red legs was shot but it was agreed not to shoot greys until a density of 18.6 pairs per square kilometre was achieved. By 2009, the final year of the project, some greys were taken as the stock was big enough. The sight and sound of a big covey must have been so thrilling.

With this crash course about wild greys under my belt I was ready for the Duke of Northumberland's hugely informative talk, entitled 'The Revival of the Grey Partridge'.

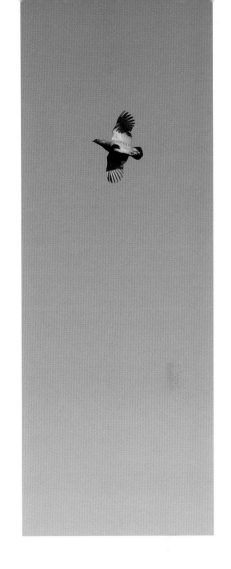

# THE RECOVERY PROJECT AT RATCHEUGH, ALNWICK

More than 200 of us listened agog as the Duke described the awe-inspiring achievements in conserving the grey partridge species at his home farm, Ratcheugh, at Alnwick.

'I am no expert on the grey partridge but I am passionate about it and incredibly lucky to have had the opportunity to help revive this little game bird's fortunes in Northumberland over the last few years and to vaguely understand it and be enchanted by its courage and beauty, thrilled by the sport it provides and to eat as many as I like! The grey partridge is in serious peril but with a bit of help it could make a comeback.

'As a boy I was lucky or spoilt enough to spend as much time as possible chasing every sort of bird. In those days five brace of walked-up greys was a real red-letter day. For much of the last century, grey partridges had a particularly hard time at Alnwick – my father and grandfather were passionate fox-hunters and the fox was protected like a deity. Rearing pheasants was the keeper's role and vulpicide (the killing of foxes) was heavily discouraged. Through the 1970s, 1980s and 1990s, the partridge, along with other farmland wildlife, all but disappeared under an intensive farming regime with big fields, few hedges, no headlands and more or less complete lack of predator control.'

it was essential to do everything possible to protect them. By 2006, they counted 1,148 birds in the autumn and Ralph and a team of Guns were able to shoot a bag of eighty-six brace of partridges and quite a lot of wild pheasants. That was an Alnwick partridge record.

Since then, 125 brace were shot in a day with single guns in 2007 so the partridge area was expanded to about 6,000 acres, looked after by three keepers. The home farm is still the core project but with the support of the tenant farmers, who have allowed cover crops to be planted along their headlands and also keep an eye on the partridges, it has been able to develop over a larger area.

When the birds pair up in January most of the grass margins are pretty bare and some of the headlands can be crushed by snow, so winter-feed is provided. Holding covers of fodder radish, kale, dwarf quinoa, stubble turnips and mustard are vital, as are the hedges and rough corners. From late May onwards the chicks will be hatching and they need lots of insects for at least the first fortnight if not a month – sawfly larvae, caterpillars, bugs, hoppers, beetles and ants in particular. On an intensive farm, enough of this important protein can be only be provided in the headlands where there must be a rich source of weeds and other plants that nurture insects. Alnwick's headlands have insect-rich brood rearer cover consisting of red millet, reed canary grass, sweet clover, lucerne and chicory, undersown in a tritikale crop in the first year for nesting cover, feed and protection.

The problem comes when the farmer wants to spray his crop. Herbicides kill the insect-rich weeds but modern pesticides are much more damaging; tiny droplets drifting into headlands can destroy most insect life and the chicks will starve. Because the cover is high by then, the problem only becomes apparent when the crop is harvested in August/September and the Duke said that it can be galling to see a few barren pairs where there should have been coveys into the teens or twenties. Consequently a twelve-metre spray exclusion zone is now set in every field, i.e. the headland plus another six metres into the crop.

After harvest, the autumn counts start. Every brood is counted and marked on a plan and Ralph and his keepers work out whether there are enough to shoot. The calculation is relatively simple – they assume they will lose fifty per cent of the post-shooting stock to mortality and migration over the winter and

Ralph then explained that his farm is located close to the A1 and the East Coast main railway so it is now too dangerous for hunting. Thus he had a clean canvas to start a relatively modest conservation project. He admitted his ambitions were fairly half-hearted because there was too much vermin, pesticides were still sprayed and by 2002 there was little improvement. But there were a few more farmland birds, even a few more partridges.

In 2003, a new head keeper, Garry Whitfield, arrived and with him came renewed enthusiasm. It was agreed that eleven miles of hedgerow should be planted, beside which six-metre field-margins would be left and sown with suitable grasses and crops for nesting cover, feed and protection.

Early headland grass mixes of cocksfoot and timothy became overgrown with clover and weeds, so these were replaced with a finer pollen-nectar mix containing sheep fescue, chewing fescue, crested dogtail, and common bent grasses with a mix of birdsfoot trefoil, knapweed and oxeye daisy wild flowers. Predation control was stepped up, 1,800 hoppers were installed at 200-metre intervals in every hedgerow, with a little tin dusting shelter and a tunnel trap. Sprays were diverted from headlands, tractors avoided crushing nests and combines stopped working at night and thus wiping out broods tucked into the corn. With only fifteen pairs of partridges to work with

they would aim for, say, 500 breeding pairs the following spring, so 2,000 birds must be left at the end of the season. That way, in theory, the surplus can be harvested – a relatively small proportion. In 2010, 700 birds were shot, more or less reflecting the size of the surplus.

Reducing migration is a challenge. Gradually the farming system is being adjusted, with more spring crops being grown and more over-wintered stubbles left. It is hoped that as new hedgerows and other measures mature, there will be less migration and pair counts will continue to improve. Millet, maize, aniseed, and small seeds mixture have also been added to the spring hoppers which should be more enticing than just wheat.

This new farming regime is a long and costly process. It has undoubtedly reduced the home farm's profitability; and better predation control has created a rabbit population explosion, annoying other farmers in the area and necessitating more time and cost to mitigate its effects. The hoppers are feeding every pigeon and crow in the area and raptors, particularly sparrow hawks and buzzards, are on the increase. But, on the plus side, independent bird surveys over the years have demonstrated an amazing reversal in the fortunes of many threatened farmland birds generally. Of the twenty-one species monitored over the ten year period, all increased except skylarks, which are abundant anyway. Breeding lapwing continue to increase, breeding blackbirds have increased by around 500 per cent, dunnock are increasing gradually, robins and wrens did well in early years but were hit hard

*Above*
*The Duke of Northumberland, who has had*
*great success with his grey partridge recovery*
*project at Ratcheugh, on his*
*Alnwick estate.*

The Somme Shoot in Rutland was the winner of the prestigious
Carter Jonas Grey Partridge Trophy in 2009 for its conservation
work to save this iconic farmland bird.

during a couple of bad winters. Tree sparrow numbers have increased into a nationally significant population. Chaffinch, goldfinch and reed bunting are all doing well; yellowhammer numbers are up 800 per cent. In addition, three pairs of sedge warblers and several corn buntings have been seen in the last two years.

The project's success was recognised by Natural England who, under the Higher Level Stewardship scheme, gave significant financial support. Not only does this help to mitigate the loss of farm profitability but such national recognition and the consequent publicity is an encouragement to other local farmers to apply to join HLS.

The Duke of Northumberland finished his talk by summing up thus:

'We have found over the course of the seven years that wild partridges respond well if limiting factors are removed, habitat is good, insects are allowed to thrive, there is enough year-round food, predation is controlled and the weather is not too awful. Above all, a dedicated keeper – or team of keepers – is the most important factor in the successful management of wild ground-nesting game birds. Seven years is not long; we certainly don't know it all and are constantly trying new things and learning from our experience and the experience of others.'

I asked him toward the end of the 2011 season how it all went.

'We shot four days with bags of fifty, sixty, eighty and eighty brace respectively. Not quite as good as hoped but we had an awfully wet summer. But with a bigger stock than ever before I hope we reap the rewards in due course!'

Another ducal estate has had similar good fortune, too. The Duke of Norfolk won the Purdey Game & Conservation Award in 2010 for his partridge restoration project on his South Downs estate at Arundel in Sussex. His achievements were reported in several magazines. Evidently, he was advised in 2002 that English partridges would become extinct on his land by 2005. Evidence to back up this gloomy outlook came in 2003, when only three pairs were counted. The duke resolved to reverse the prediction. He reviewed every aspect of his farming operations, put a good team of keepers in place and planted fifteen kilometres (just over nine miles) of hedgerow. By 2007 he was ready to enter Natural England's Higher Level Stewardship scheme,

*Above*
*Our Irish host for the day at Raby with*
*his faithful friend at his heel.*

*Roy Rayson at the Somme Shoot in Edmondthorpe.*

designed to seek maximum environmental benefits for wildlife from targeted sites across England as we have seen, and his application was successful. By the autumn of 2009 the count revealed 2,150 English partridges in residence! A subsequent shoot saw a bag that included 291 grey partridges and 305 red legs (plus 42 pheasants) – all wild.

But it is not just big farms and estates who embrace grey partridge recovery projects who witness rewarding results. Landowners with farms of all sizes can be involved in the process and prove that you do not need thousands of acres to make an impact.

# A 400-ACRE PROJECT IN LINCOLNSHIRE

Having heard and read so much about these amazing little game birds I was ready to see some and I didn't have to go far. I visited Gerald Needham one late summer evening on his farm at Coleby on the Lincoln Cliff, a portion of a major escarpment that runs north-south through Lindsey and Kesteven in central Lincolnshire.

Gerald is extremely passionate about grey partridge restoration and he has tailored his farming approach on one of his farms, which is 400 acres, for their benefit. His efforts were recognised when he was presented with the Game and Wildlife Jas Martin Silver Partridge award at the Lincolnshire Show in 2011.

His passion is shared and supported by his wife, Lizzie, and their three daughters, Kate, Holly and Harriet, who are now all in their twenties. The girls are not only keen shots but also avid followers of the local Blankney Hunt and have all ridden to hounds at some stage in their lives and continue to do so. The whole family shares an interest in and enthusiasm for the countryside and the pursuits it offers.

Driving around in the back of Gerald's 4x4 to see grey partridge restoration plans in practice, I expected to see multiple coveys of partridges all over the place. I guess that is my commercial shoot instinct but whilst we didn't see any on this occasion I am assured they are here! I am learning to be patient. Gerald has counted almost a pair for every twenty acres in 2011 and he is expecting further greys to pair up in January 2012. He has a theory: if the weather is fine for the Lincolnshire Show – usually held during

the third week of June – and vermin is controlled effectively, you will hopefully have a good partridge-breeding season.

Despite strong land and no spring cropping he has observed a successive 100 per cent increase in grey partridge numbers for each of the last three seasons. Not just greys either but more linnets, finches, songbirds, buzzards, sparrowhawks and carrion crows: more stoats, foxes and weasels.

The farm spreads across the heath from the top of the Lincoln Cliff to the flat land beneath it. I must have mentioned my daughter, Violet's, eighteenth, which prompted Gerald to recall a great day's shooting they had had on the farm and in particular a wonderful shooting drive over the Cliff for his daughter, Holly's, eighteenth birthday. She had a few friends to shoot and they bagged eighty-one birds, twenty-three of which were wild greys. How special is that?

The Needhams shoot four days in a season and bag in the region of 70-100 birds. At present Gerald releases 400 pheasants, which he keeps well away from the greys, which he says are more likely to flourish if they are left alone. He usually gives two of the four days to his daughters and hosts the others himself. But he doesn't actually shoot at home. He takes pleasure in watching the birds and all the action from the beating line, which he runs himself. 'That is,' he admits, 'unless so many greys appeared that I'd have to join the Guns.'

He is adamant that without the Entry Level Scheme in 2006 and then the Higher Level Stewardship scheme from 2007 none of his improvements to the partridge habitat would have been possible. The support has been invaluable although he admits that now, even if it were to be withdrawn, he would carry on anyway. But so far the schemes have helped him to plant many new hedgerows and trees on the farm, an ongoing process. Other measures include field margins surrounding all the fields and twenty-metre wide coverts down the full length of his fields with kale, chicory, sweet clover and phacelia for nesting and brood-rearing. Throughout winter he feeds grey partridges from strategically placed feeders in hedge bottoms. After the greys have paired up, each pair has its own feeder that he restocks right through until May.

Gerald has done all that he can and more to provide the perfect habitat on his farm for not only grey partridges but for a wide variety of wildlife. He has been resourceful with what his land has to offer. Even a disused railway has been transformed and enhanced to provide dense game cover. He has also dug new ponds, which are surrounded by newly planted vegetation and used for duck flighting.

The sun starts to set and as we make our way back to the house Gerald spots a strange vehicle parked up in a field. 'Poachers!' he roars. He drives up behind the car, flashes his lights and gets ready to jump out and tackle them. Only these trespassers weren't after game – they were half-naked, steaming up the windows and enjoying their own entertainment! Undaunted, Gerald still wrote down the car's registration number.

Back at the house we sit round the kitchen table with Lizzie for a drink and look through the game book. One particularly fine entry records: '1998, 2 November, 150 grey partridges'. This just proves there need not be a shortage of greys if they are cared for suitably.

# THE SOMME SHOOT IN RUTLAND

Another wild grey partridge shoot local to Belvoir is the Somme Shoot at Edmondthorpe in Rutland. John Pochin, whose family has owned the estate since 1761, invited me to visit in late September prior to an October shoot.

In the late 1980s, John's father, Anthony, died and as John took the helm he resolved to farm the land that had been let to tenant farmers. A childhood memory of shooting wild greys in north Norfolk also made him determined to try to establish greys at Edmondthorpe. He advertised in Norfolk for a keeper in 1993 and met Trevor Ash, who was then working for Lord Buxton. Trevor took the job and is still there today. Sandra, Trevor's partner, whom I remember meeting on a sponsored ride at Belvoir once, has since trained to be a keeper too and now works alongside him.

Everything and everyone is immaculate; keepers are smartly dressed in family tweed and a feeling of great pride in the shoot is tangible. We are right on the Rutland-Leicestershire border with Lincolnshire, a county which has been associated with English partridge since the days of the late, great Sir Joseph Nickerson (about eighty miles to the north-east of here). He was considered to be one of the greatest

shots – ever – and liked to shoot 100 days per season. In times gone by big bags of wild partridge were legendary there, with the record an unbelievable 2,119 wild partridges shot in one day. Today his nephew, David Nickerson, runs a 7,000-acre estate of undulating arable and grassland near Rothwell, tucked away in the heart of the Lincolnshire Wolds.

But those halcyon days took place well before modern farming methods had been introduced. Thankfully, there are growing numbers of passionate shoot owners like John who are undaunted by the challenges and are prepared to farm their land less profitably but with the least cost to wildlife in general and the grey partridge in particular,. On my visit, John had asked his agent, James Goodson from Fisher German, to join us and I sensed that perhaps he had

been puzzled initially that anyone should jeopardise their farming revenue for anything, let alone a wild bird population. Such an opinion might well be shared by his accountants too, but John regards grey partridges and other wildlife as part of his farm income.

Fortunately, Natural England, as we have seen, supports a merry band of English partridge disciples like those at Edmondthorpe and along with the GWCT and the stewardship schemes offers advice and funding for projects. Success is as much about problem-solving as it is management and every wild partridge shoot has its own particular difficulties.

For starters, the heavy land here in Rutland is not ideal for greys as they prefer light and sandy ground. Little partridge feet get clogged up with wet clay in the winter and they struggle. They suffered too

*Above*
*At the Somme Shoot: from left,*
*head keeper Trevor Ash, me,*
*John Pochin, assistant land agent*
*Matthew Pocock, Sandra Baines*
*and James Goodson.*

in 2011 from a particularly warm and dry April and there weren't enough insects for the birds to eat when they hatched and many were lost.

But looking back to when it all started at Edmondthorpe in 1991 with twenty pairs of wild grey partridge arriving from Walsingham in Norfolk you realise this is a success story on many levels. Only two years ago (in 2010) enough of a surplus had been established to shoot 205 birds one day and 187 on a second day with double guns and everyone present; John, Trevor and James know this was only achievable due to unimaginable patience, time, excellent keepering and hard work. It certainly wouldn't tick the boxes for a commercial shoot but this isn't just shooting *per se*; this is purist sport for the ardent traditionalist.

As in many similar shoots, a large percentage of John's land has been planted with wild bird mix for summer brood-rearing cover, while other areas are seeded with a different mixture to provide winter food supplies and shelter. They also use a split-field system. James Goodson explains:

'The original idea of the strip fields was to emulate the old four-course rotation of winter and spring crops with grass land being used as a break crop. With the combination of the four crops being drilled in one field, it was hoped to provide a year-round food source and cover for the grey partridge.

'The current strategy is six strips within each field averaging one hectare to one-and-a-half hectares in size, which are generally treated in the same way as the other commercially grown crops on the farm. The strips are made up of winter wheat, winter beans, overwintered stubble to be drilled with triticale and lucerne and second year lucerne.

'Each separate crop is split by a six-metre strip of either game maize or canary grass, with the twenty-four-metre headland area being sown down to grass. The last six-metre margin to the hedge is sown with a cocksfoot stewardship type mixture.'

Over time, mixtures have changed and developed as Trevor, the agronomists and Fisher German have found what does and doesn't work – a sound principle that is adopted on the rest of the shoot too.

After years of experimenting with breeding programmes Trevor thinks the so-called Montebello System works best, in which pairs are selected and forced together in small breeding enclosures in the hope that they will take to each other. If all goes to plan

*Opposite page*
*The Guns and some of the beaters on my day at one of the country's premier wild bird shooting estates,*
*Lord Barnard's Upper Teesdale Estate at Raby Castle:*
*third from left, Robert McKergan, second from right,*
*the editor of* The Field, *Jonathan Young, and to his right,*
*head keeper for 35 years, Lindsay Waddell. Sitting down,*
*keepers Andrew Hyslop, James Watson, William Makepeace,*
*and Richard Dodd who was beating for the day.*

*Above*
*Guns can be challenged by the topography as birds are driven over the steep slopes at Cotterdale.*

and chicks hatch, they are released at three to four days old with the adults into suitable habitat where an eye can be kept on them.

Insects for the chicks to eat (usually for the first ten days or so after hatching) should be in abundance from the many acres of insect-inducing wildflower mixes that have been planted. Fallen trees are left to lie because they make wonderful fortresses for a whole host of insect life. Then there are beetle banks, an idea developed by the GWCT in collaboration with the University of Southampton. Tussocky grass like Yorkshire fog, cocksfoot, crested dovetail and timothy, is planted next to a raised bank the full length of several large fields to allow great numbers of predatory ground beetles to become established. Good nesting cover is provided for game birds too and if the system works properly farmers shouldn't have to spray harmful insecticides either. Another pivotal moment in a wild partridge's life, as we know, is during harvest and John's contract farmer is good enough not to combine during the night to protect the birds.

Each spring, pairs are counted and then again postharvest. They expect to lose fifty per cent of their stock over winter. In order to work out how many they can shoot and to protect breeding stock they deduct the number of pairs they require for the next year from the August count and allow for the winter losses. They will only shoot a surplus. No surplus – no shoot.

As an 'island' shoot, with no neighbouring wild grey partridge shoots, there is another problem in that the greys inevitably stray over the boundary, especially

as the Pochin land backs on to a commercial shoot at Stapleford Park near Oakham. Stapleford has a policy not to shoot greys but Guns can and do find it difficult to identify them in the excitement of a drive. Some will inevitably get shot.

Trevor and Sandra have given me some idea of their roles and nothing less than total dedication is required. For the last eighteen years they have not had a holiday, choosing instead to commit their lives to the farm and the shoot. They start their morning at 5am, walking the dogs, setting traps and snares to control vermin and checking everything over, finishing their day in the same way. With a boss who matches their drive and ambition they make a formidable team. It is quite clear that without this level of determination, sustained over twenty years, it would be a different story here.

Before I left we all jumped into the Land Rover for a guided tour. All the drives are named after battles fought in the First World War. We see all the hedges that have been planted; the tall brood-rearing cover growing in six-metre headland strips in every field; the beetle banks clearly defined and lots of grey partridge in pens and dotted about in coveys.

On my way home I was thinking how we could try and create a natural habitat at Belvoir for wild grey partridges and I think the perfect spot would be at Croxton Park, three miles from the castle. Plans are already afoot to restore a derelict hunting lodge on the site and my mind is whirring with possibilities.

When I return on 24 October 2011 to see the shoot in operation I meet Fraser Thomsett, a keeper with Lord Romney in Norfolk and loader for my dear Herefordshire friend, James Verdin, aka Jimmy the Grouse for his prowess in a grouse butt. Another Gun, Julian Romney, has waited thirty years to shoot wild partridge on his shoot on farmland near King's Lynn and now he has retired he has set up the north Norfolk partridge group. No one is here by accident.

John hands out the game cards, all illustrated with pictures of classic cars from his collection – another hobby – and including a full list of all the rules for the day.

The shoot is run as a syndicate and each of the eight Guns knows John well and cares about grey partridges as much as he does. They shoot six or seven days a year and apart from a few pheasants will shoot only wild greys. Everyone understands how special these

*Above*
*Inspecting her quarry....*
*Six species after the first drive at Raby*
*with Lindsay Waddell.*

*Below*
*A covey of greys approaching the line.*

*Standing with Jonathan Young, editor of* The Field. GREY PARTRIDGE & WILD BIRDS 71

days are and if too many birds look like being shot, they stop.

Bruce Seymour, the keeper from Stapleford Park, joins the beating line: it is so reassuring to see neighbouring shoots working together like this. I am to be placed behind John's son, Simon, on the first drive of the day, on an old canal that doubles up as a duck drive. I know from proud Dad that Simon shot his first wild grey partridge aged only 14 (in 2010), so he shouldn't feel under too much pressure today I hope.

Once on our way in a spotless trailer – which reminds me that ours needs a jolly good clean up before the start of our season – the adrenalin starts to pulse through everyone's veins.

We are told that when you hear the whistle a covey is on its way. Within minutes of the start the whistle blew and hey presto, what a sight, as a huge covey of partridges bursts over the line like rockets, darting left and right and diving low over the hedges. This is such challenging shooting sport.

All goes well, the birds are picked and as we walk back to the Guns' bus I see a face I recognise. 'Good morning, Your Grace, bullshot?' he asks. And then I place him: it's Roy, one of the pickers-up and loaders at Belvoir. He is a member of the Somme Shoot syndicate. I apologise for being rather lost in my own little world with all these grey partridge and offer to load for him. He tells me he is coming up for his eightieth birthday in a few weeks and had shot for years at Belvoir in one of the early syndicates. Watching him nailing one grey after another it is clear he hasn't lost his touch.

Edmondthorpe is a prime example of how this sort of management can influence wildlife for the better and many organisations, as well as Natural England, bring visitors to see how it's done. The estate's success was also recognised by the Grey Partridge Recovery Project, which is run by the GWCT, when sponsors Carter Jonas presented the prestigious Carter Jonas Grey Partridge Trophy to John in 2009 for his conservation work to save this iconic farmland bird.

Wild bird shoots clearly have a special quality to them. So far I've visited grouse moors and grey partridge shoots but I have had an invitation from Lord Barnard to experience a multi-species wild bird day – on a two-day back-to-back shoot – at Raby Castle in County Durham.

# A WILD BIRD SHOOT AT RABY CASTLE IN COUNTY DURHAM

Lindsay Waddell, head keeper on the Upper Teesdale Estate for thirty-five years, runs about three days a season that are let to long-standing clients. This is one of the premier wild bird shooting estates in the country, covering about 35,000 acres of which 16,000 acres is moorland, and it is a great honour to be here. Today there are six Guns and six beaters. I team up with Jonathan Young, editor of *The Field*, whom I hadn't met before but liked enormously. I thought he might be the perfect person to ask about shooting etiquette. He had much to say on the subject and very kindly agreed to summarise some essential guidelines for me, which you will find on page 97.

We make our way to the first drive and crouch behind a stone wall. Two Guns are above us in the line and three others are walking up. For the record, there was a howling gale with horizontal rain which all contributed to what our photographer for the day, Rupert Watts, summed up as 'real seat-of-the-pants shooting'.

Jonathan, dressed in full camouflage regalia, is as excited as a child on Christmas Eve. He thinks we may see duck or snipe first. Within seconds, cue beaters, and a shout of 'Snipe!' Short pause. Bang. Gentle thud. The beater's shrill call provides a stark contrast to the orderly tapping of sticks and sedate rustling of flags on any shoot I have been on before. Here the quarry is awoken and evicted with a start. With no certainty of type, or numbers to follow, no one is expected to miss.

As a spectator you really feel the true wildness of the whole event. Two mallard suddenly appear from the boggy land in front and fly into Jonathan's sights and those of his neighbour. Two more down. As the tension of the wait intensifies, so the appreciation for the birds multiplies. Where have they come from? Some will be from the immediate vicinity and others could be from as far away as Poland or Germany. Very occasionally a bird will have been ringed in a foreign country and this illustrates a fascinating journey here via the Northern Flyway. At the end of the first drive, Jonathan hands his bird to Mr Waddell, increasing the tally to ten. There are now six species in the game cart

*Left*
*Good feet positions are*
*not always guaranteed.*

already: one grey partridge and a Frenchman, snipe, duck, grouse and rabbit.

I join Lindsay Waddell himself on the next drive. I have heard so much about this man and was really looking forward to meeting him. He has been a gamekeeper since he was sixteen, served on the board of The Nature Conservancy Council (now known as Natural England) and was a founder member of the Moorland Gamekeepers' Association, formed in 1982 to provide guidance for keepers in the uplands. Then in 1997 the National Gamekeepers' Organisation was founded by a group of gamekeepers who 'felt that their profession was threatened by public misunderstanding and poor representation' and the two groups merged (see the NGO website for further information). Mr Waddell is the current NGO chairman and explains that it is an organisation run by gamekeepers, for gamekeepers. It has approximately 16,000 supporter members of which about 5,000 are keepers themselves.

The work they do to defend and promote gamekeeping and maintain standards is invaluable but I was really struck by a new training course that the NGO offers to police forces, free of charge. Rural crime on shoots is so easily misunderstood, as we have seen in the grouse chapter. The course is structured to help officers distinguish the many subtle differences between legitimate and illegal practices in the countryside. In under a year, since the first training session started, fifteen forces across the country have benefited. One officer subsequently reported that he had been able to make a clearer judgement about a gamekeeper's use of a trap, which spared an unnecessary prosecution.

*Lindsay Waddell and myself at twilight at the end of the day.*

# PHIL BURTT'S TOP TIPS FOR WILD BIRD SHOOTING

## WALKED-UP WILD BIRDS

Whatever wild game you are shooting be prepared. Wear good walking boots and dress for the day bearing in mind you may be walking five miles or more. Wear light, thin layers that you can peel off.

Always take a drink and something to eat.

Always be at the ready when you are walking up with a loaded gun. It is very easy to have your gun under your arm when your chance to shoot a bird presents itself and you will miss it.

Bearing in mind that you may cross brooks, dykes and fences, be ready to unload your gun and check that the barrels are clear before reloading. Safety is of more paramount importance on these days than perhaps any other.

Don't shoot something you're not prepared to carry home yourself. There isn't always someone close by who can take it for you. So don't pull the trigger if you have too much already.

## DRIVEN WILD BIRDS

Shooting reared or wild birds is a relatively similar experience but remember that wild bird instincts make them much more observant than the reared bird. They are older, wiser – and wild! Don't talk; keep the noise down on approach, as they are acutely aware of their environment and will know if you're there. They will always catch you out if you are not ready.

---

Let us hope that this initiative signifies some progress towards the beginning of an end to an awful lot of painful accusation that can threaten the livelihood of a shoot and its staff.

But back to the shooting. Another difference on this shoot from any others that I have been on is that after several hours there are no breaks. No elevenses, no lunch, no nothing: not yet, anyway. Still it rains and still it blows. Mr Waddell confers with the head beatkeeper and we head for higher ground that results in a calculated and perfectly executed cull of several grouse. The day's species list is growing.

I'm not one for flagging but after three long drives it was a relief when someone suggested a brief rest. My nearest companion was Robert McKergan, who told me how he knows everyone here today. They all met nearly twenty years ago at an Irish Game Fair in Belfast and have shot together regularly ever since. Mr Waddell, known to Robert for many years, let him know when an opportunity for a day became available at Raby and the group took the chance without hesitation. Robert and his beautiful German pointer work hard all day and the synchronicity between them is a joy to watch.

The day continued much as it had started without losing any of the drama or energy. The bag at the end was the total for two days of shooting, back-to-back (I was there on the second day): 26 pheasants, 2 brace of grey partridge, half a brace of French partridge, 12 and a half brace of grouse, 6 woodcock, 5 snipe, 14 duck (including mallard, wigeon and teal), and 8 rabbits.

It's a worry when you write about a shoot that you may not do it justice but Mr Waddell has helped me. He has written a book of poetry, with a foreword by Jonathan Young, called *A Gamekeeper's Reflections*, a vivid portrayal of a lifetime spent looking after gamebirds. One of the poems that describes the magic of a wild bird shoot is called 'The Wanderer':

I cradle its body in my hand,
It's from a far, far distant land
Perhaps a thousand miles or more
Before it crossed this foreign shore.

What has it done? What has it seen?
Where was it going? Where has it been?
O'er the sea in the dead of night
Certainly not an easy flight.

The full moon lighting the stormy wave –
Many a life that light will save.
Escape they must winter's ice-like grip
Over the sea and south they slip.

Where it was going who can tell
Before it to my own gun fell
Down to earth it did gently land,
Didn't turn out like this bird planned.

From river mouth to mountain top
On they go, they seldom stop,
Driven to leave by an ancient urge
On and on in a feather surge.

In case the winter makes them pay,
That's the reason they must not stay,
And in my hand this one's at rest
The sportsman's prize, the very best.

The sportsman has a duty of care
To watch over those who he does slay –
Respect we must those lives we take
We should not kill for killing's sake.

It seems to me that part of the excitement of wild bird shooting is inevitably about trying to predict the unpredictable, which keeps everyone on their toes. At the beginning of December, Gerald Needham emailed me from his Coleby shoot, and summed up the whole chapter for me.

'On Tuesday we shot at home. The instructions to my friends were no greys [on the land that Emma had looked round]. On the first drive after lunch we went to a thirty-acre field of over-wintered stubbles with three acres of wild bird cover, on Navenby Heath. With a good west wind, seven Guns were placed at sixty yards apart and waited in anticipation for ten beaters to start. The drive lasted only fifteen minutes. I only had to look at everyone's faces afterwards to know something extraordinary had happened. Up to seventy greys were seen bursting over the hedge. Four brace were shot plus four brace of red legs. Good friends, Mark Harrison and Tom Tunnard, achieved a left and right; for Tom it was his first ever.

'This is what shooting is about. The results are not inspiring in commercial terms but hard work and dedication does work but you have to have passion.

'Regards, Gerald.'

# 4

# RED-LEG PARTRIDGE

PARTRIDGE SHOOTING SEASON
1 SEPTEMBER – 1 FEBRUARY

When David and I moved into the castle in 2000 we took the bull by the horns on pretty much everything. We knocked the private apartments into family accommodation, we got to grips with the estate, modernised and updated as much as we could and worked out ways to develop the shoot. It was suggested that if we introduced more partridges we could extend the season and thus increase our revenue. Yes, of course the shoot needed to make money, but more than that I am a great believer in promoting our sporting heritage and sharing it with a wider audience.

The red-leg partridge, or Frenchman, is a big part of our shoot today and I have a lot of respect for the species: they may be the poor relations compared to their revered and smaller grey cousins but along with pheasants provide the backbone for much of our country's game shooting and have provided marvellous sport on all types of land, including those flat land areas where it is impossible to get reared pheasants to fly at sporting heights.

I once overheard someone in our shoot room expressing the view that the Romans first introduced the red-leg to our shores. Apparently Charles II did too, when he acquired some from Spain for target practice. After a bit of digging around on the internet I learned that in 1770, the Earl of Hertford imported eggs from France to be reared by chickens on his estate near Orford in Suffolk, and it was then that the birds really became established. It also explains why they are known as French partridge.

# A LOW-GROUND PARTRIDGE SHOOT IN LINCOLNSHIRE

To further my research I was invited to a partridge shoot near Sleaford in Lincolnshire by Tim Dean, who has been farming nearly 2,000 acres there since the 1990s and running his own shoot for twenty years. The land in this area of Lincolnshire is typically light and perfect for growing vegetables, root crops and oil seed rape – the last of these Tim plants straight into stubble to create ongoing cover, and partridges love eating it too. I notice that all his hedges are over ten feet in height and he explains that because the landscape is fairly void of reasonable hills and natural contours he leaves them

like this to 'lift' the birds to a sporting height.

He puts down about 10,000 red-legs and 1,000 grey partridges a year. But, I say to him, I thought you couldn't rear the two types together because the birds are so territorial and the dominant red-legs push the greys away? 'That's true,' he replies, 'but I have been buying English for twenty years from a Danish game farm and see no reason to stop now!' Sometimes, I guess you don't need a complicated explanation. And the practice seems to work, at least at the beginning of the season. It certainly adds to the thrill of a drive if a Gun has got his eye into red-leg coveys and then some English partridge suddenly appear, frantically darting about on their own.

Tim runs the shoot with father and daughter keepers, David and Sarah Boynton. Just as I was enthusiastically launching into my sentimental spiel about families working together, the Guns arrived. The day has a good feel to it. The early October sun is shining, the wind is a good south-westerly and the atmosphere, even though I hadn't met anyone yet, felt very welcoming.

The Guns were part of a roving syndicate who had all met in a pub in Beaulieu in the New Forest nearly a decade before and vowed to shoot together in different places every year. Incredibly they had been true to their word and although a few of the personnel have changed, Tim Dean's shoot is a date in the syndicate diary that is never missed. Arthur Wardman, the syndicate organiser, is first in the lodge with some of his party and thankfully he doesn't mind me intruding on the day with a photographer, a notebook and a barrage of questions.

It's the first day of their season and many of them have had a big party in a nearby hotel the night before so they are ready for some fresh air. There is Lawrence Bolton who runs a flower stand in London, Iain Wardman, who started shooting only the previous year, has a renewables business, while Arthur himself is a retired engineer. The rest of the team I will meet as the day unfolds but they are all excited to be shooting again. Just before we set off for the first drive, Tim talks us through the rules of the day. There will be five drives; no ground game is to be shot; leave cartridge cases at your peg; leave game behind your peg for the pickers-up; listen for the whistle to end the drive; you can shoot English partridge if you see them but, finally, don't shoot any pigeons before game on each drive because it will spook the partridges. All this sounds very reasonable.

We make our way to the Guns' bus; an ex-police

riot van bought just after Arthur Scargill had led the miners through their strike in the 1980s. Once we are all sitting comfortably I lean over to Tim and ask why he has to explain the rules every time if they are regulars? I get a look that suggests I must be out of my mind. He explains patiently that no matter how many times people have shot in any particular place, it is a duty of care to remind everyone about safety – and etiquette. Shoot managers and owners expect everyone to respect the safety rules and to be polite. One of the most common pictures in any shooting enthusiast's downstairs lavatory must be the Bryn Parry illustrated poem *A Father's Advice* by Mark Hanbury Beaufoy:

If a sportsman true you'd be
Listen carefully to me…

Never, never, let your gun
Pointed be at anyone…
That it may unloaded be
Matters not the least to me.

When a hedge or fence you cross
Though of time it cause a loss
From your gun the cartridge take
For the greater safety's sake.
If 'twixt you and neighbouring gun
Bird shall fly or beast may run
Let this maxim ere be thine
'Follow not across the line.'
Stops and beaters oft unseen

Lurk behind some leafy screen.
Calm and steady always be
'Never shoot where you can't see.'

You may kill or you may miss
But at all times think this:
'All the pheasants ever bred
Won't repay for one man dead.'

Keep your place and silent be;
Game can hear, and game can see;
Don't be greedy, better spared
Is a pheasant, than one shared.

*Opposite page*
*David Boynton, Tim Dean's*
*keeper for ten years,*
*with his spaniels.*

I stand with Tim on the first drive at the top of the line. Before the whistle has blown a stunning covey of wild greys craftily escape to our left. But they have gone and no one got a chance to shoot. But suddenly it's all action stations and clouds of partridges are whipped up in the wind and dart over us at over forty mph with the wind behind them. The high hedges act as essential props as the birds are forced into the sky for some truly competitive sport.

The Guns are good. As I catch up with Mr Boynton after the first drive, I ask how many? 'Two hundred and forty-two shots fired', he answers, 'all on the counter.' How many birds were bagged remains to be seen.

For the next drive I'm travelling with the beaters and I note that the average age is probably about seventy. I sit next to Ernie, who is eighty-two, and if the combined age and experience in this one vehicle tells me anything about longevity, it must be to keep doing what you love. And they all do love beating and being part of the shoot, as simple as that – and why wouldn't they?

Lunch, after the second drive, is in a converted barn and cooked by Tim's girlfriend, Amy, who is a professional cook. We pull up our chairs for a feast of Lincolnshire sausages (made by local butcher Robert Mountains in Boston), served with onion gravy, Tim's carrots and peas from the farm and just enough wine to kick-start a flow of stories about various infamous and notorious characters – oh, and requests for a good caravan pitch at the next CLA Game Fair, which we are hosting at Belvoir in 2012!

With several pitches earmarked for my new friends, it is to my chagrin that I have to leave after lunch but what a wonderful shoot and such great people. I was particularly struck by the dedication of Mr Boynton. Nothing fazes him; he's seen it all before and yet appears to see everything with fresh and infectious enthusiasm: he has real wisdom.

# A SHOOTING CO-OPERATIVE IN SUFFOLK

With red-legged partridge having originated in Suffolk it seemed appropriate to visit a shoot in the county but unfortunately this wasn't possible. But I did have the pleasure of an in-depth conversation with a man who has developed a very clever syndicate.

*Left*
*A really fun bunch of Guns who managed to talk me into giving them the best caravan pitches at Belvoir Castle when we host the 2012 CLA Game Fair. We are pictured leaning up against the Guns' bus. Tim Dean is on my left.*

Stephen Partridge-Hicks, known to all as SPH, bought the splendid Little Haugh Hall, set in sixty three acres of parkland, eight miles east of Bury St Edmunds, in 1998. Seven years later he acquired a further 800 acres and keeper Robert Frost came as part of the deal too. The shoot was well run and provided modest sport, 'but, frankly,' said SPH, 'it wasn't big enough to cover its fixed costs.' So having never run a shoot before he concluded that either the keeper would have to work for much less, or he would have to scale it up.

Luckily, he has good neighbours and this is where it gets interesting. He approached Richard Ballard, who owns 400 acres next door in Pakenham, who agreed to join forces. Other neighbouring landowners, Robert and Stephen Honeywood, Peter Hay, and Bill Baker (and in some years John and Roger Catchpole and Charles Mathieson) each had sufficient acreage and interest to combine, thus extending the shoot to cover 3,500 acres. This provides enough land to run a sizeable shoot from which all can benefit, with more drives and bigger bag days – and, as a cooperative, none of the negative politics that can arise between individual neighbouring shoots.

Partridges are well suited by the undulating low ground in the west Suffolk uplands but to 'break' the landscape SPH planted four miles of hedges and five new woods named after his five children, two daughters and three sons. What a lovely idea. The older children, now in their early twenties, are keen shots too and join the line of Guns when they can. Dad hopes to have an entire line of PHs at the Christmas family shoot one day. Maize, dwarf sorghum, mustard and sunflowers make up some of the cover crops, which provide shelter and feed for the partridges and add to the biodiversity of the land.

With five branches to the cooperative, how does it all work? 'Everyone can leave their own front door and shoot over the combined land on their shoot days. I prefer a formal shoot with a relaxed atmosphere and invite all our Guns to bring wives, girlfriends and children to stay for a weekend. Some like to go beating, others might stand on pegs but I like to see everyone outside enjoying themselves,' says Stephen.

That sentiment sums up the whole sport: to have fun and enjoy some good shooting in beautiful surroundings with a great bunch of mates.

# A GUNDOG FIELD TRIAL

I may not have managed to spend a day with SPH, but one event I did participate in was the two-day Midland Counties Labrador Retriever Club Open Qualifying (Any Variety) Stakes at Belvoir Castle. This meant nothing to me until I learnt that all gundogs and their handlers aspiring to enter the hugely prestigious International Gundog League Retriever Championships must first qualify and this field trial was a part of that qualification process.

The organiser, Mrs Deborah Green, is by coincidence the wife of Dr Chris Green, who has helped me a lot with farming decisions at Belvoir. She tells me that one of the advantages of being involved in countryside pursuits is that the participants get the chance to see beautiful parts of the country that might otherwise remain closed to them.

My own understanding of gundog training is limited. I grew up with obedient spaniels and labradors but apart from trying to instil some basic discipline into my beloved cocker spaniel, Janie, when I was a teenager and making sure the dogs at home are looked after, training as such is not my forte. We've got chocolate coloured mutts galore: a chocolate labrador called Nelson; a liver cocker spaniel named Belvoir; Daisy, a liver-spotted dalmatian and Susie the shih tzu. Before our children were old enough to go shooting the dogs were just family pets, but since shooting has become the number one priority in the holidays, the dogs have become the subject of much amateur training. Nelson, who is now six and arguably too old to train, has surprised us all and learnt a lot, but Belvoir, then aged one, was ripe for proper training and we sent him to Frances Brookes for some expert tuition.

I have to admit that I had never attended a trial before and I was amazed to see at least sixty vehicles parked in the car park. I was introduced to all the judges, Mr Stan Tweedy, Mrs Arlene White, Mr Gordon Hay and Mrs Jennifer Hay and some of the show members, who were observing the trial as part of their show judge certificate. Every age group seemed to be represented too, which was lovely. Central to proceedings was the club's president, Mrs Joan Hayes, a local lady who has bred and handled more field-trial champions than you can wave a walking stick at. Her father owned and trained Staindrop Saighdear, the first yellow labrador to qualify as

*Above*
*Tim Dean discussing the next*
*drive with David Boynton.*

*Above*
*Competitors awaiting their turn.*

*Opposite page*
*A successful retrieve.*

a 'dual champion' (that is a champion of field trials and also on the bench) and was the Kennel Club's Dog of the Year in 1947. Including him there have been only three dual champions since the Second World War.

Deborah Green gives the following wonderful account of the day's events in her club report, which appeared in The Midland Counties LRC Yearbook 2012 (reproduced here by kind permission of Midland Counties Labrador Retriever Club). It sounds terrifyingly competitive but all in good heart!

The head keeper at Belvoir Castle, Tim Rolfe, the Steward of the Beat, lined out the 'Guns' and first competitors in a field of rape with the end Gun on the far side of a wide belt of woodland, out of sight from the majority of the 'field'. The first retrieves were made on that side of the trees and then a pheasant was shot on the near side of the wood allowing the gallery to watch Mr Worral's dog, Oakvalley Black Storm, make a neat retrieve, ignoring a hare that flushed right in front of him. He followed this with another retrieve behind the line of Guns.

A pheasant was shot which landed just inside the line of trees. The only Golden Retriever in the competition, Vamp Parsley Pottage, successfully retrieved this bird after having a little difficulty negotiating a wire fence hidden in the thick undergrowth.

The action slowed after this for the observers as several dogs were 'tried' on a long, running bird that disappeared into trees on the other side of the belt. As the judges also failed to find the bird, these dogs remained in the competition.

At the end of the field, the line of Guns turned and worked up the far side where every one could see the action. Everyone was willing one competitor to retrieve a running partridge. The determined dog worked well but unfortunately was called up before it could find the game. At this time we were treated to a display by some RAF training planes that buzzed the field several times, seemingly interested in what was happening.

We stopped for a lunch break and then moved to a new piece of ground. A strip of maize cover was located in a valley bottom between two sloping fields. The Guns lined out on each hill, either side of the maize and shot birds as they moved forward. The gallery had a good view of all the action. A pheasant was shot a long way behind the line and four dogs attempted to find it but failed. As the judges had no difficulty locating the bird, all four dogs were put out. Several dogs including Heather Bradley's Heathergaye Hundall and Richard Beckerleg's Staverton Nicky found birds easily in the maize crop while others had difficulty on a pheasant falling behind the hedge at the top of the hill.

By the end of the first day the judges decided to keep only twelve dogs in for the second day. Everyone adjourned for the evening.

Heavy rain fell during the night but the day started bright and sunny. We returned to the belt of trees and the rape field where we had started the previous day but instead of walking this up, the Steward of the Beat, Tim Rolfe, decided to line the Guns out for a small 'drive'. Birds would fall into the advanced oilseed crop and make interesting retrieves allowing good hunting and use of 'nose'. All twelve dogs stood in the line and the birds were shot in short bursts allowing time for retrieves on either side of the wood. By lunchtime several dogs had been put out for failing to make a retrieve.

After lunch we moved to a fresh piece of ground; oilseed rape bounded by hedges on three sides with a strip of young oats and a cover crop of maize. Four more dogs failed to make a retrieve which the judges found leaving five dogs in the running for the awards. The birds were becoming harder to find and we still needed several to finish the trial. Mr Hales' bitch Delfleet Ptarmigan successfully negotiated a long retrieve before we moved again to new ground. Lowforge Aragon of Leacaz handled by Lee Hartis made light work of a difficult retrieve through a hedge before 'eye-wiping' two other dogs on a pheasant shot fifteen yards beyond the hedge on the opposite side of the field. Just when the plentiful supply of game seemed to ebb, a large flush appeared from the end of the hedge where two of the Guns were positioned to provide all that was needed. A head-to-head battle was then waged between the two contenders for first place, Lowforge Aragon of Leacaz and Mr Jamie Bettinson's Whitesmiths Widgeon. It was a difficult

*Above*
*Guns take note: this handler*
*has seventeen spaniels with him.*

*Opposite page*
*Competitors in the two-day Midland Counties*
*Labrador Retriever Club Open Qualifying (Any*
*Variety) Stakes at Belvoir Castle.*

decision but Whitesmiths Widgeon was finally awarded the honours of the day which made him a Field Trial Champion. Lowforge Aragon of Leacaz was a close second, winning Guns' choice, with Mr Philip Down's Amancio Thunder and Mr Robert Worral's Oakvalley Black Storm both being awarded Certificates of Merit.

In the late afternoon, as the long crocodile of vehicles left the car park it felt almost as if we had had a proper day's shooting, albeit shooting with a difference. Historically the estate has always been very happy to help facilitate the valuable work that trials achieve and it was a huge privilege for me to witness the event first hand. Field sports rely heavily on dogs' instincts and training and without these trials and championships many skills would be lost.

# A HIGH-GROUND PARTRIDGE SHOOT IN WENSLEYDALE

Now that I had learnt about two low-ground partridge shoots, Phil Burtt was keen to show me how these birds fly over high ground, so took me to the edge of a grouse moor to witness this for myself. Cotterdale (part of the Simonstone Estate, which includes Stags Fell) is near Hawes in Wensleydale and lies on the lower side of High Abbotside moor. It is a relatively new venture and was bought by Michael Cannon fifteen years ago for grouse shooting. He owns other moors too, including the world-famous Wemmergill (see Chapter 2). At Cotterdale, along with his friend and co-owner of Stags Fell, Richard Johnson – who plays a big part in the moor's management – they have developed a shoot that I had already heard just goes from strength to strength.

On my visit, a group of Lincolnshire businessmen and farmers had taken a day and were due to gather the night before at nearby country house hotel, Simonstone Hall Hotel near Hawes, also owned by Michael Cannon. This pretty market town overlooks the North Yorkshire Dales where nothing can have changed much since veterinarian James Herriot walked up hill and down dale to treat sick animals, and difficult owners.

Jim Gale, the agent who had organised the day,

whom I know well because he brings lots of parties to Belvoir, was at the hotel's door to meet me as I arrived first thing in the morning. Head of the party was Rick Hall and his son, Rob, who together run Hall and Hall, Britain's leading restorers of vintage racing cars, in Lincolnshire. I'm always interested in the demographic of shooting parties and Rick's team of close friends was no exception to the general rule that people from all walks of life love shooting. Amongst them were builders, mechanics and farmers; some faces I recognised from shooting at Belvoir and some I knew as friends. I was introduced to Alan Singleton, who is semi-retired and hosts days at Cotterdale in Richard Johnson's absence, and somehow we got on to the subject of etiquette. One of Phil Burtt's pet hates is bad manners in the shooting field. It is a difficult subject because the word 'etiquette' tends to imply a snob element but actually in the case of shooting, it is mostly about safety and remembering to acknowledge the many people in the background who have helped to create the best day's sport for a team of Guns. Fortunately, as I have said, I managed to corner Jonathan Young (editor of *The Field*) on a shoot at Raby Castle and asked him to write his essential list of dos and don'ts for good shooting etiquette. You'll find his invaluable advice at the end of this chapter.

Fiona Robinson of Whaupley Gundogs (who is also the Simonstone estate secretary), was out with her gorgeous working cocker spaniels. Our eldest son, Charles, has a spaniel called Belvoir which was sired by one of Fiona's dogs, Whaupley Scarp.

We make our way to the first drive and pick up our list of shoot rules, which includes the instruction 'no black grouse'. They are protected here, as they are in many places since numbers started declining over a hundred years ago and more dramatically from the early 1970s. Cotterdale supports the Black Grouse Recovery Project and the estate receives grants to improve their habitat. Anyone who shoots one, even by mistake, is fined £500.

There is a red squirrel regeneration programme here too as some of the land forms part of the Widdale Red Squirrel Reserve, and on the way to our pegs we saw at least one possible nesting site in the hollow of a tree, lined with bits of bark. I didn't realise that red squirrels still existed in the UK, other than ones that have been reintroduced, but this area is one of the few places left where they still thrive and one of sixteen

*Left*
*Trainer and handler Lee Hartis with Lowforge Aragon of Leacaz (aka Bob). They came second at Belvoir and won an Open Stake a few days later. Bob is now a Field Trial Champion and qualified to run in the International Gundog League Championship.*

*Top left*

*The Guns at Cotterdale: Rob Hall*

*(second left) and his father Rick*

*Hall (third from right) had taken*

*the shoot on the day I visited.*

important Red Squirrel Reserves in the north of England. Surveillance teams record sightings and they also set up clever feeding devices in woodland that double as data collection sites. Enticed by food, hungry squirrels enter through a tube – hopefully losing a tiny amount of their coats along the way – and then make a dash for the tasty morsels in the feeding tray at the end. Hair samples are then collected later for analysis. Obviously most reserves require the support of landowners and this is certainly one where everyone is keen to help.

The head keeper, Mark Rennison, runs twenty-five let-days a season and a few family days for Mr Cannon. Mark and his under-keeper, Stephen Millman, release 18,000 birds a year that have arrived as poults in the summer. But managing the birds for shooting is just the tip of the iceberg. Over the last fifteen years, Mr Cannon has invested fortunes on High Abbotside and Cotterdale by heather reseeding; thinning out congested tree plantations; replanting mixed woodland to support more wildlife and erecting new fencing. Like many new shoots, the workload is never ending. In addition to the two pheasant and partridge gamekeepers there are two moorland gamekeepers, Paul Starsmore and Amy Lucas, who undertake predator control on an area which extends to about 10,000 acres.

Joining us today are fifteen beaters and five pickers-up, who I notice are all very young and look exceptionally fit! With the steep terrain ahead of us youth is probably an advantage. Looking at the weather as I get out for the first drive, I'm betting it will rain. What is that old saying? 'Rain before seven, fine before eleven.' Well there was no rain before seven this morning so we may not be in luck.

I am standing with Tony Dighton, who has a son in the same year as our youngest, Hugo, at school, and we're chatting about rugby when birds suddenly start to scream across the valley high up over the top of the trees on the Coal Syke drive. Pheasants, partridge, woodcock all just whiz over high above us, whilst all you can hear is shot after shot accompanied by peals of laughter. Out of 235 shots fired only 35 birds are bagged. Anyone who connected with a bird is right to feel very proud.

As we get back to the Guns' bus it starts to rain. I met a lovely chap, Robert Mudd, walking to the second drive called Tarn Gill. He may have been seventy-four but he was nipping along the line picking up any spent cartridge cases around the pegs like a man possessed. I offered to help him. I think I'm quite fit, I run most days and I watch what I eat, but Robert strode off in front of me with all the youthful energy of the young beaters and he was always at the next peg before me. So how does he do it, I ask? 'Clean living; no smoking; no drinking and plenty of Yorkshire air.' Fair do's, I'm beaten on all counts.

Its elevenses and out comes a beautiful walnut box full of glasses from someone's car-boot for champagne and sloe gin. I light up a shameless but necessary cigarette. Everyone is full of enthusiasm about their day and the height of the birds and of course, as always, the many, many birds that got away.

For the next drive I'm beating with the head keeper, who is definitely the sort of keeper you wouldn't mess with. He has a no-nonsense, let's-get-on-with-it manner for which I have great respect. We push on to the start of the next drive, onwards and upwards over ever increasing contours of a hill that seems to have no apex when he says, 'the worst problem I have up here is losing trees in the wind'. As I pick my way over one fallen trunk after another where the trees have been wrenched out of the ground by their roots by the freak force of nature, I can see the problem. I am growing increasingly grateful for a wet day and not a windy one.

Another drive provides even more thrillingly high birds. Before Michael Cannon's involvement this was just a fairly ordinary hill in an extraordinarily beautiful place. Now the shoot is the epicentre of a thriving community, the land heaving with wildlife and properly managed to maximum effect. Back in the bus with the beaters I have another chance to further my research into the demographics of everyone involved in shooting and I ask what they all do. Amongst them there are plumbers, builders, someone on work experience and a policeman on his day off: again and again I am meeting people from many different walks of life but all of them have one thing in common – they are devoted to the countryside.

Lunch is taken in a magical stone building on the side of the moor. Simonstone Hall Hotel seems to have come to the lunch hut – a feat in itself. I have been constantly struck by the attention to the decorative detail in shoot lunch huts. Here there are trophy heads of game on the walls, a generous drinks sideboard, a

huge dining-table and comfortable chairs; a gas stove, crystal glasses and silver on the table, plus a Polish butler and a local chef. Lunch is a veritable feast over which to salivate, with pudding and an extensive cheeseboard, the deliciousness all washed down with very good wine. You could be in a top London restaurant not stuck on a hill somewhere in the Yorkshire Dales.

Everyone has shot really well and it is decided to shoot only one of the two drives in the afternoon. The final bag includes partridges, pheasants and one grouse, every one of them as sporting as the others. Then it was back to the hotel for yet more food: scones with jam and cream, cakes, Earl Grey, China and Indian teas, all of which you can happily tuck into because you have walked off half your body weight since stepping out of the car that morning!

All my visits to grey and red-leg partridge shoots have been a revelation. Hosting commercial shoots at Belvoir is a wonderful privilege but I didn't really understand how these birds actually live. Now I have a much clearer appreciation of the skills you need to shoot them as well as a little more awareness of the skills needed to present the birds to the Guns in the most sporting way possible. And best of all, while I can see that a coveted wild grey partridge shoot is the result of huge investment, time and patience, the comparatively humble red-leg can create some pretty stonking sport too.

# GOOD SHOOTING ETIQUETTE,

## BY JONATHAN YOUNG,

### EDITOR OF *The Field*

1   Always reply to shooting invitations immediately, by phone or email, and confirm in writing. Once you've accepted, don't change horses for a better invitation.

2   Find out exactly what's required. Some invitations will require double guns and black tie. If in any doubt, ask.

3   Take plenty of cartridges and a lot of cash Borrowing is a bore. If your dog is wild or whickers, leave it at home. If it's a weekend party, take your host a present.

4   Always arrive ten minutes early. Make certain by leaving far more time than the journey normally demands. Have your host's mobile number to hand in case the motorway is closed.

5   Make a point of introducing yourself to the other Guns and chat to the keepers, pickers-up and beaters. Do your level best to remember that 'shooting party' comprises two words and don't overlook the 'party' bit. As a guest, you have a duty to your host to help make sure it is an enjoyable day.

6   At the shoot briefing, listen carefully to how the Guns number. Do they move up two or three? From the right or the left? And what's on the menu? Some hosts prefer to leave woodcock unshot. Many have a 'no pigeon before the gamebirds' rule. And some do or don't want you to shoot foxes (I always look the other way when Reynard passes). Make certain you know the signal for the start and end of the drive.

7   At the peg, carefully mark the slice of sky that defines your birds and stick to those. If a bird would make a better shot for a neighbour, then let it pass. Don't poach unless you know each other extremely well and then do it only once – and don't do it all, even if the fellow Gun is a bosom pal, if he's having a thin drive. It is especially heinous to steal birds off the young, the elderly and lady Guns. If your neighbour misses with both barrels, then you can attempt to wipe his eye but be careful you don't do this too often. People get annoyed. The situation is more complicated with grouse and partridges shown in the English style, low over hedges. Hesitation is fatal, so get stuck in on the coveys but leave the singleton that's obviously your neighbour's bird. If you wound a bird, kill it with the second barrel rather than swing onto a fresh bird.

8   Keep an accurate tally of the birds you've killed and mark where they've fallen. Mark especially carefully any you have pricked. At the end of the drive, pick up those around the peg and give the picker-up precise instructions as to how many remain to be picked, and where they are.

9   When you tip the keeper, congratulate him on the drives that went well and always take your grace brace.

10  Send your thank-you letter as soon as possible and try not to make it a boring bread-and-butter job.

## PHIL BURTT'S TOP TIPS FOR PARTRIDGE SHOOTING

The thing to remember with all partridge shooting is that a good bird isn't always a high bird. A reared French partridge always produces a good sporting target whether it is high or low: one isn't necessarily more difficult than the other.

---

Partridge hug the contours so don't shy away from a low bird – assuming it is a safe shot.

*Above*
*A well-behaved gundog is welcome on*
*any shoot but if it isn't cutting*
*the mustard, or worse is out of control,*
*Gun and dog could both lose an invitation*
*to come again!*

# 5

# PHEASANTS

PHEASANT SHOOTING SEASON
1 OCTOBER – 1 FEBRUARY

No one really knows when the first pheasants were shot for sport. There are stories that suggest Henry VIII may have done so in the early 1500s but certainly as flintlock guns developed in the mid-eighteenth century walked up shooting started to become popular. The 3rd Duke of Rutland's flintlock gun, on display in the Guard Hall in the castle, leads one to believe that he was probably shooting game at Belvoir from the early 1720s. Our game books start in 1800 but a recent archive discovery of a 1734 document, a 'bill & receipts for the carriage of 20 pheasants from London to Belvoir – Waggon to Grantham then footmen to carry 'em to Belvoir £1:6s:1d' could either have been for a banquet or possibly for breeding stock. The 3rd Duke's wife, Bridget, died in 1734 and perhaps he was looking for new ways to fill his time.

Belvoir's topography offers a great mix of high and low bird drives to suit everyone, including complete beginners. But over the last few years there has been a general trend for people wanting to shoot really high birds and Belvoir has its fair share of requests for such challenging sport. I like to think, though, that shooting is – and will always be – a 'gentlemanly' activity (for both men and women). Fortunately, on all the shoots I have visited, every bird is as special as the next.

# CAERHAYS IN CORNWALL

One of my visits was to Caerhays, one of the top pheasant shoots in the country, where there is no shortage of quality birds. But to tell this story properly I have to go back eight years. I was struggling to get to grips with various ideas for the gardens at Belvoir when I met Charles Williams at the Chelsea Flower Show in 2003. One area that was proving particularly difficult to plan was our woodland garden and no one, to my knowledge at least, has a more interesting, historical or captivating woodland garden than Charlie at his family's home, Caerhays in Cornwall. His great-grandfather, J C Williams, was one of the first to plant rhododendrons, which had been brought back from China by the great plant hunters, E H Wilson and George Forrest at the very beginning of last century. By 1911 JCW, as he was known, was sponsoring Forrest's third expedition and the seeds he came home with that time have grown into magnificent plants that bloom spectacularly every year.

Today, the 120-acre garden is a fabulous example of traditional Cornish spring planting and home to the world-famous National Magnolia Collection.

Rather cheekily, I suggested to Charlie that he might like to donate some plants to Belvoir and use our garden as a central England outpost for his nursery business but he told me, without an iota of malice, to **** off. One of the things I love about him, as well as the glint in his eye, is his straight talking. Despite turning me down, he has become a wonderful friend and his advice about gardening, estate matters and our shoot has been highly sought after and highly respected. He is a champion of many a good cause and well known for throwing his no-messing support and common sense behind countryside issues for BASC and the Countryside Alliance. He is not afraid to stand up to Defra either, if necessary. Apart from that, he and his wife, Lizzy, are great fun and terrific company.

The Caerhays pheasant shoot, originally a twelve-day family affair, is now an eighty-day commercial shoot plus his private days and its success has been a great source of inspiration for us at Belvoir. Lizzy has restored a completely derelict Georgian rectory, The Vean – and installed a chef – for shooting party accommodation. And together with Charlie's character looming large over the day and the hugely rugged topography, which drops away to the beach, Caerhays has become one of the best and most sporting pheasant shoots in the country.

Charlie was born and bred at Caerhays Castle and the grounds were as much a home to him as the John Nash-designed Regency building that was bought by his ancestors in 1860. As a child in the 1960s, entertainment was a bit DIY albeit supervised by various estate staff. Charlie and his brother were regularly issued with hessian sacks and packed off to neighbouring farms to collect broody hens and bantams as a way of amusing themselves, as sadly their mother was ill with multiple sclerosis. The way he tells it, it was obviously fun but at the same time he was acquiring a deep understanding about the countryside – not just from the keeper, but also from the gardener, woodman, cowman and anyone else he came across on his travels around the estate. He has managed to instil similar rural values into his children and they were only allowed to shoot after spending at least two weeks with the keeper to learn about rearing.

He returned from a successful banking career in the City in the 1980s and set about running Caerhays with its 4,500 acres, 140 houses and family shoot as a

*Opposite page*
*High speed action in the field.*

business. Farming was changing and his land, which is mostly down to grass now, was turned over to grazing for sheep and cattle that can survive some of the cruel winter weather that lashes against the Cornish coastline. He employed a new keeper, Patrick Coombe, who was with him for thirty years, and upped the number of birds dramatically. Today, with the help of head keeper, Philip Tidball, he has 3,000 Kansas hens and cocks in the rearing field supplying 100,000 eggs a year. He sells 20,000 and sets the remainder at Caerhays to produce 65,000 chicks of which he will expect to have 40,000-ish really good birds to shoot, from 1 October. He also puts down 5,000 partridges and there are a few resident wild greys and wild birds. Early birds are released into a valley to keep them together. He swears by the belief that you shouldn't shoot a pheasant before it is 23 weeks old.

Tellingly, Charlie has very few days at the beginning of a season to sell. His prices vary depending on the bag but he charges (in 2011) about £34 per bird plus VAT, which is less than I expected. He reckons you need to entice people if they are to travel all the way to Cornwall, although the new airport at Newquay has certainly helped many clients. It is not uncommon for helicopters to be seen landing on the nearby beach or in the gardens but that is yet another expense for a Gun.

Charlie Sainsbury-Plaice, my photographer for the trip, and I stayed with Charlie and Lizzy, and Charlie's parents, in the castle. Over dinner the night before the shoot, I met a great lady, Bettie Town, aged eighty eight, who bred and handled champion English setters from the Sharnberry kennels. She won the Pointer and Setter Champion Stakes several times in the late sixties and seventies and she and her setters were well known on many grouse moors at that time. Bettie is still keen to pick up and will be out with us in the morning.

Waking up early to write my notes after rather a late night felt somehow less arduous in a beautiful if rather extraordinary circular room, with glorious views over Porthluney Valley and the sandy coves at Portholland. Smugglers were well known along this coastline and tales of shipwrecks and all the local history add a touch of mystery, evoking scenes from the wonderful *Poldark* novels. In fact much of the subsequent television series was filmed here. With no mobile phone signal you could be forgiven for feeling transported back in time. At 6am the early dawn was casting long shards of gloomy light through the eerie mist in the valley, as an old cock pheasant was calling out in the park – there is always an

*Right*
*One of Lizzy Williams's many*
*perfectly trained labradors in*
*action.*

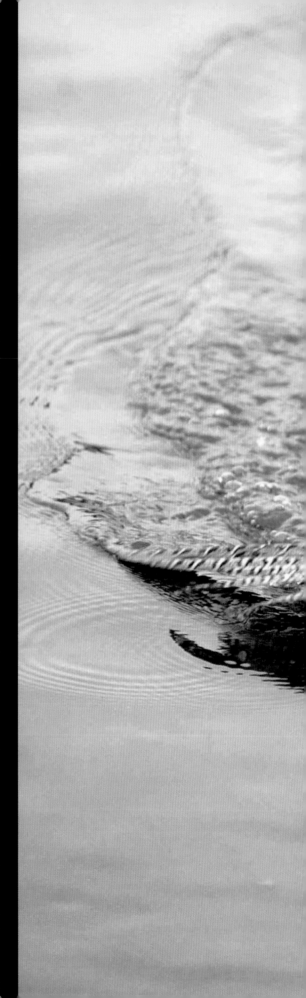

old cock pheasant in these scenes! But the peace was shattered as six black labradors pounded their way down the corridor outside my door. It was time to surface and start the day.

The shoot began with everyone gathering outside the front door for instructions. I was dressed from head to toe in fur and some of the Americans in the party, who have been coming to shoot at Caerhays for thirty years, looked rather alarmed. (Note to self – consider dressing down off home territory.) But after lots of banter in the Guns' bus everyone relaxes. Patrick Mackay has organised the day with a team of friends from New York. He knows some friends of ours in America and soon we are all chatting away, with shooting of course the common interest.

The first drive is Hanging Wood Drive and Charlie shows me all the trees that he has planted in his forestry programme with the help of various government grants. (He has a reputation on the estate for making full use of all the available benefits and is sometimes known as Charles 'Grant' Williams!) Then there are the cover crops: some are wild birdseed mixes grown as part of Natural England's Countryside Stewardship Scheme (soon to be superseded by the Environmental Stewardship scheme). All the grants help to make the shoot profitable, which ensures employment for local people and thus does its bit for the local economy too. So here we are on the first drive, with spectacular views of the garden. When I visited in the spring it was ablaze with colour from rhododendrons, azaleas, magnolias and camellias, but now it is teeming with pheasants. I asked the head gardener, Jaimie Parsons, how he felt about his precious gardens being over-run with shooters every winter but he is reasonably relaxed as long as no one tramples on the young camellias.

I imagine that in grounds like these even dogs might respect the garden and find one of the few trees of nonarboreal interest for a quick pee. Three dogs that look as if they would never put a foot wrong, never mind cock a leg against a fine specimen magnolia, belong to Tricia Watson. Her black labradors are beautifully trained, amongst the best I have ever seen. She told me how she had come over from South Africa aged eighteen to train to be a musician but met and married her boyfriend forty-five years ago and has been here ever since. After her children grew up she started breeding and training labradors and as well as

training dogs for other people is out picking up between fifty and sixty days a season.

But it was Patrick Mackay's loader who really caught my eye on the next drive. Alan Campbell has all the confidence and ease with a Gun that is only achieved through years of experience. He is crucial to the shoot because when he's not loading he is looking after the shot game for pretty much all of the eighty-two days. Why? Because, he says, 'It's a beautiful and idyllic place, you see some really excellent shooting and there is a very friendly family atmosphere – even at the end of the season. And Mr Williams looks after us very well.'

On the third drive I join head keeper Philip Tidball's wife, Sheila, with the beaters. She is sporting a very jaunty cerise pink knitted hat which I am quietly coveting. Sheila and the under-keeper, Jack West (who has just completed a gamekeeping course at Sparsholt College, near Winchester in Hampshire) encourage me to stick to the path so as not to get my feet too wet.

Another stunning drive, on the cliff top above the beach, is over and with the beaters I make my way back to the castle for lunch. Everyone is very relaxed. I was chatting to a very elegant blonde-haired lady in the beaters' cart who has retired from nursing and now loves to spend her time beating. The fifteen beaters and pickers-up enjoyed a roast beef and Yorkshire pudding lunch in the tearoom. 'Well fed beaters are happy beaters' is Charlie's motto.

I don't know how he runs this shoot with only three keepers but the answer, I discover, is in the tearoom: volunteers. With great diplomacy Richard Wain runs a team of pickers-up and is out nearly every shooting day. John Burford has been helping the keepers for the last twenty-two years. Bob Turner has helped for regular ten-week stretches for the last six years. John Bidgood has been beating for eight seasons and is devoted to the shoot. All the beaters are paid £15 a day and Charlie gives them two beaters' days at the end of the season, to which they all look forward. The keepers have three days, and everyone is happy. He puts much of his shoot's success down to the continuity of exceptionally good staff. They know what they are doing and Guns keep returning to shoot at Caerhays.

I take my place in the castle's grand dining-room for lunch with the Guns in front of a blazing fire, surrounded by portraits and stuffed trophy heads of game on the walls. A shoot lunch of roast lamb with vegetables and sticky toffee pudding will set us up for the afternoon. I sit next to Lizzy and Leslie Baker, who was an insurance broker in Cornwall and managed all the insurance for the Williams family. When he retired he offered to host the shoots and with his gentle manner and soft Cornish accent is perfect for the role.

Lizzy is as passionate about Cornwall as Charlie and has supported many local craftsmen during the refurbishment of houses on the estate. Everything in the once ruined old rectory, The Vean, and fourteen redundant farm buildings on the estate, has been painstakingly restored into holiday accommodation, the work being done by local people and the rooms furnished by Cornish suppliers.

Despite the gloom of our present economic climate Charlie and Lizzy employ nearly a hundred local people to work on the farm, garden, nursery, houses, shoot and building business. This shoot isn't just an example of exemplary management borne out of a deep understanding of the countryside, it is also a perfect example of a shoot pulling the community together to showcase local talent and skills to all its visitors. I felt proud to be part of our shooting fraternity.

# WILL GARFIT'S SMALL SHOOT IN CAMBRIDGESHIRE

By way of a complete contrast, my next visit was to an award-winning small shoot in Cambridgeshire. Pigeon-shooting enthusiast and wildlife painter Will Garfit invited me to see for myself the shoot that he runs on just eighty acres in the middle of an urban sprawl between the M11, two villages and the main London-to-Cambridge railway line.

When Will bought the land forty years ago it was a disused gravel pit and the surrounding area nowhere near as built up as it is now. As he welcomes the Guns with a quick talk at the beginning of the day he mentions that the concrete has edged a little nearer, but to me this just seems to emphasise even more the beauty of his little oasis. I hand out the game cards for him and note that they are printed with the wildlife scene from the cover of his first book, *Will's Shoot*. The shoot has won the prestigious Laurent Perrier Award

*Above*
*Sharing a joke with*
*Charlie Williams.*

(now the Purdey Award, of which he is a judge) and on the back of each card is a list of press comments from all the shooting magazines as well as *The Daily Telegraph* and *The Times.*

Will has proved that on just eighty acres you can produce up to nine, 100-bag mixed game-bird days – in a good year – by putting down 750 pheasants and 150 duck and successfully managing the wild birds. He runs the shoot purely to entertain his many shooting friends and to repay their hospitality. Nearly all of them have been coming for years and have seen Will develop the shoot from nothing, with the help of the keeper, Brian Morley, and ten beaters.

After a quick coffee and a sip of Laurent Perrier champagne to toast the award's memory we walk to the first drive – there are no vehicles. Dogs, beaters and Guns all walk together to their positions. I meet a chap who is sporting a very dashing Rupert Bear type waistcoat and he corners me about 'this book I am writing about shooting'. I sense that he seems to know what he's talking about which makes me a little nervous. When Will tells me later that he is John Humphreys, the great countryside and shooting writer and author, I'm grateful for not putting my foot in it – or maybe I did!

We start the first drive of the day, Triangle Drive, next to an area of maize in front of a new housing estate. The beaters stand with their backs to the houses and beat the birds towards the Guns. Will points out his tree-planting strategy intended to present the best sporting birds by growing a commercial crop of specimen trees next to the maize. The birds take off from the game crops and keep flying very high up over the trees to the willow woodland where the Guns are placed. It seems to work extremely well. The beaters then gather to flush through the wild privet in front of the line. Will explains how this holds the birds before they are driven over the Guns.

The second drive, Maskell's Drive, is named after Dennis Maskell, the postman who owned this five acre field before Will bought it. Dennis had kept bees and Will had a good arrangement where he would swap honey for a brace of oven-ready pheasants.

We all wait while a fox scurries from the maize and one of the beaters, Bernie Sewell, reminds me that a pheasant takes off from the ground at a cost of £27.00 to the shoot owner and comes back down with a value of £1.00 to a game dealer.

Elevenses includes a blast from the past as I'm offered a Wagon Wheel. I haven't eaten one for years and they're delicious. Very fitting too, as when you stand still you can hear the wheels of the traffic thundering up and down the M11.

For the next drive I had the pleasure of loading for John Humphreys and now that I had got over my nerves I warmed to him instantly; very sadly, he passed away shortly after this memorable day. He was a Welshman too, which is an endearing characteristic for this Welsh girl who is trying to learn all she can about shooting in one season. And who better to teach me, because John was a schoolmaster and started writing about shooting when he retired and clearly had so much fun and enjoyment from his brilliant second career. In between offering support for my book project, talking about my children and his grandchildren, he shot everything that came over him.

In no time at all it was the midday break and we assembled in a former industrial building for a tangy tomato soup with a dash of sherry and some Melton Mowbray pork pies, all washed down with a cocktail of champagne and sloe gin. On the wall was a list of every Gun who has shot here over the last forty years and it reads like a list of the shooting world's *Who's Who*. Then it was time to move on to the next drive by the lake, with a limit of up to eight shots at duck per Gun. I stood next to Tony Cooper, who has known Will for years through mutual friend Archie Coats. Tony only ever shoots with a 28-bore but doesn't miss a thing. He really is a dead-eye Dick.

We must have seen nearly a hundred duck and a woodcock. Surrounded by woods and looking over the lake one could have been anywhere. You had to remind yourself that you were actually sandwiched between industry and urbanisation of one sort or another.

One of the beauties of a small shoot is that you don't need to drive but walking around a small area that is heavily planted can be rather disorientating. The diversity of the wildlife was astonishing: we heard so many songbirds and a muntjac suddenly appeared, hurled itself into the lake and swam to the other side. This was pretty unusual, as apparently muntjac don't like swimming. It's hard to believe that this little piece of rural England won't be engulfed one day but its survival is thanks to Will Garfit. It is a great example for anyone who aspires to running a shoot on a small scale.

At the end of the last drive, beaters and Guns catch up to discuss the finer elements of their day and lay out all the game for everyone to see. Will sees this

ritual as a mark of respect for the quarry, which has given everyone such sport. The results, he suggests with a smile, must have something to do with his friends being inspired by the duchess as it's a particularly good bag: 105 pheasants, 45 mallard and 1 pigeon, total 151. Another ritual is for the Guns, having thanked the beaters, to disappear smartly to a local pub for a hearty late lunch.

*Above*
*Will Garfit in characteristic*
*jovial mood.*

*Above right*
*A rare sight, a muntjac in the water.*

*Right*
*At Will Garfit's shoot in*
*Cambridgeshire – he is on my right.*

# WESTWICK IN NORFOLK

Inspiration comes in all shapes and sizes. I have been unbelievably fortunate in being able to visit some truly awesome shoots over the last year, for which I have mostly to thank Phil Burtt for opening his address book and diary. Together we visited his old friend, John Alexander, at Westwick in Norfolk for a shoot in late November. If I had to pick a handful of the most extraordinary days of my season of discovery, this would be one of them.

John, despite a brief early incarnation as a musician in the late 1960s (the shoot still attracts many of his old well-known music friends) has been passionate about shooting all his life. His father, Sir Alex Alexander, was a friend and shooting companion of the late Sir Joseph Nickerson. As a boy, John very often just happened to be in the right place at the right time – usually during lunch on a grouse moor – for first-hand lessons about fieldcraft and shooting skills from the great man, Sir Joseph, himself.

So what is the Westwick shoot like? Norfolk is usually associated with flat to undulating land and I have always thought it more suitable for partridge shooting. Westwick, on the north-eastern corner of Norfolk, despite its beautiful timeless setting of parkland and woods, has a landscape that is rolling rather than flat. I know Norfolk people can get a bit uppity when their undoubtedly glorious countryside is dismissed as 'flat' because it really isn't. The Fens are flat, Norfolk is not, but I come from Powys and anything close to sea level can look steamrollered to me. I tell you now though: I was a fool to think it mattered.

We climbed into the Guns' bus – a former mobile library vehicle – and headed off to the first drive. Just as everyone was making their way to their pegs a red deer sprang through the maize cover crop, followed by a muntjac nipping about in front of the Guns. I picked up a hint of frustration from my host, who wasn't shooting, choosing instead to stay with the beaters. I stood with Wally French (father of top eventer Piggy French) and we waited for the start of the drive. I still doubted that the birds were going to be very high. How wrong I was! A convenient tree plantation, grown specially to create the maximum

effect, sends the pheasants soaring into the sky and for about an hour no one stands still for a minute.

John has the attitude of a perfectionist and I'm detecting that he's happy but still thinking how the drive could have been even better. I admire that approach and he appears to care deeply about every detail as well as enjoying being in charge. No one is allowed to drive their own vehicles and mobile phones are frowned upon. I wasn't allowed to join the beaters' line for a chat either because he thought having a furcoated duchess wandering around gossiping would distract them from their task. He also pointed out that a shoot like this can only work if it is run with military precision, so no, I had to do as I was told and keep out of the way. Quite right – point taken!

Ian Garfoot is the head keeper. He has been at Westwick for twenty-eight years with his wife, Marian, who goes out every day too. I'm longing to ask him about the logistics of this shoot but Phil keeps telling me that it is the height of bad manners to ask how many birds a shoot puts down, so I keep quiet. It is true that I have seen some vexed faces when I have asked people in the past but there we are. Some tell and some don't. And no, I didn't ask.

All five Guns are old friends and the camaraderie and banter is very entertaining. The quality of the shooting is Olympic standard. Next to me on the second drive are Stephen Padley and his very glamorous wife, Nicola, who is loading for him. The Padley family has been shooting at Belvoir for twenty years and my late father-in-law used to relish their visits. He always marvelled at the standard of their shooting and it really thrilled him when they shot huge numbers out of certain drives.

Toby Dennis was my next target for a quick chat. He and his wife, Sarah, are friends of ours from Lincolnshire. Coincidences keep growing once you recognise a pattern and none more so than amongst the people here today. Toby's aunt was married to Sir Joseph Nickerson and there is a feeling that Sir Joseph is never very far away.

The day finished with a whopping great big bag, shot by five masters of their craft – Robert Carter, Stephen Padley, Phil Burtt, Wally French and Toby Dennis. I can honestly say it was without doubt the best shooting I have ever seen and what an honour to witness such skill. I can only think that if Sir Joseph had been present he would have had a very good day too.

*The muntjac and hare that interrupted the beginning of the first drive at Westwick.*

*John Alexander the perfect host.*

# STANAGE CASTLE, POWYS

My penultimate pheasant shoot was to take me back home to the Welsh borders in Powys, for a day with the Coltman-Rogers at Stanage Castle. My boys had left the day before to stay with my parents, who live close by, and as I approached Ludlow – twelve miles from home – it started to snow. Nostalgia quickly set in, especially as it was only a week before Christmas and everywhere looked so magical. Our family farm, called Heartsease, was part of the Stanage Estate until the 1930s when my great-grandfather bought it for one of his seven children. Since then my father has expanded the acreage as well as buying the house they live in now, The Cave. (My brother and sister-in-law have moved into Heartsease, our childhood home.) Mum and Dad and my boys were all getting ready for a day out with the Rat Patrol, the local shoot that my family has been involved in for years. So after a quick cup of coffee I left them all to it and set off round the corner for Stanage Castle.

I had never been inside the castle before, despite living so close and riding past it so many times on my pony as a child. And what a beautiful day for a first visit, covered as it was in snow. I met Jonathan and Sophie Coltman-Rogers in their warm and cosy kitchen where sausages and bacon were sizzling on the Aga for breakfast. I learnt, very quickly, about all the changes in the last twenty years since I had left the area. For Jonathan, farming was not a viable option as a major revenue source on the estate so he developed the pheasant shoot in 1993 and started putting down ordinary ring-necked pheasants. The steep and dramatic topography here is ideal for shooting and with the castle sitting so well in the grounds it has great appeal for paying Guns. I hadn't realised that Jonathan's first cousin is Charlie Williams, my host in Cornwall, which surprised me because his language, so far, hadn't been littered with expletives. He has the same recognisable bonhomie however, and I had no doubt that the day was going to be fun.

I also met Jonathan and Sophie's son, Guy, who was home from Aberystwyth University where he is reading agriculture. He was going to be helping and told me that the team of Guns, all friends of the team's leaders, Bernard and Sarah Taylor, had been coming to Stanage for years. Bernard and Sarah work in the City, as do most of their party. Guy disappears with the twenty-four beaters and nine loaders and Jonathan explains the order of events. Evidently, out of a total of twenty possible drives, there will be four today: two will be easy and two more challenging but because of the snow, all options are being kept open.

Jonathan wasn't brought up to understand the countryside like his cousin Charlie and has acquired his fieldcraft skills through trial and error. Not that you'd know. There is a sense of Rolls-Royce standards here as nothing is left to chance. It's all terribly English and understated, just as I had imagined it would be.

Standing on the first drive, The Belt, with Bernard, I recognised the lie of the land instantly from my adventures with Betty, my pony. I met Mark Cole, Bernard's keeper from his home and estate, Rycote Park. Mark's family is allegedly the second longest serving gamekeeping family in the country and he is proud to tell me that he is the eleventh generation of gamekeepers and his son, already shaping up nicely by all accounts, will be the twelfth. Bernard keeps him busy loading. We are standing next to a huge crop of felled timber and birds keep appearing, each flush higher than the last, swooping, dipping, diving and giving great sport.

As we make our way back to the vehicles our photographer gathers the beaters in a gateway for a team picture. I meet Martin Pitt, one of the loaders, who does this job for most of the forty days that are let each season. He knows my father, John Watkins, and I'm getting a definite sense of recognition with many of the beaters although it is probably twenty, thirty or even forty years since I last saw some of them.

The next drive is called Ragged Kingdom and it's in Stowe Valley, which Jonathan explains is the warmest valley in Shropshire. I had always wanted to see this drive as I had heard that it was Stanage's showpiece. I stand with Sarah Taylor, who shoots with a 20-bore, and has been shooting for years with her 'if you can't beat 'em, join 'em' attitude. She does very well too, as few birds escaped her sights on the first drive. But this time she was next to a Gun who let nothing pass him, shooting dead everything that came his way, and her skills were rather redundant. Good thing that they are all old friends and take drives like this in their stride. The hot shot was Emmeram von Braun, a German friend.

*Right*
*Stanage Castle standing proud*
*on a winter's morning.*

Snow fell heavily during the next drive and Jonathan and Guy were keeping a close eye on proceedings. But their concentration breaks to introduce me to a picker-upper called Butch who, surprise surprise, is a butcher from Brecon. He drives sixty miles on every shoot day to help out. Despite the weather, the birds are soaring but I didn't know that they could be blinded by snow and that they are hovering rather than flying over the line. Consequently the Guns appeared rather perplexed at times but the drive finishes with huge numbers of shots registered on the clicker.

Lunch was a wonderful surprise for me, not least because it was in the old Stanage School house where my father had been a pupil. Sophie, with a strong eye for interior decoration, had converted the building into a fabulous lunch hut on the edge of the main road from Knighton. Potted shrimps and hot sausages from a buffet counter were all bang on the money. Sitting next to the fire gave me plenty of time to make notes and I cornered Herr Emmeram von Braun to ask where he had learnt to shoot so well. It turned out that he had been taught by an Olympic shot who, to my astonishment, turned out to be David Davenport, the uncle of my sister-in-law, Jane Watkins! I suppose I should have realised that everyone I met could well have some connection with my family.

Wrapping up again for the last drive was necessitated by the bitter weather but this didn't dampen anyone's spirits. Jonathan and Guy had ever thing under control and their teamwork was a real pleasure to witness. The day finished with everyone having taken part in some great sport both on and off the field. I found Sophie and Jonathan to say my goodbyes and to thank them for such an enlightening day. I was thinking how funnily life turns out sometimes. These charming people and their top-class shoot had often borne the brunt of our family's jokes as the Rat Patrol profited from their birds' migration to our side of the border. 'So where are you shooting tomorrow?' enquired Jonathan, as I headed for home. 'The Rat Patrol,' I smiled. 'Oh those buggers!' he laughed back at me. *Touché*, after all these years.

*Above*
*Bernard Taylor, team leader on*
*my day at Stanage, with his*
*keeper Mark Cole.*

*Main picture*
*High birds over the log pile at*
*Stanage Castle.*

# 'THE RAT PATROL'

And so there is only one more pheasant shoot left to visit – the somewhat infamous Rat Patrol. For years I had always assumed it was just an organised roundup of winged game on farms in our home locality by my father and his friends. The shoot's origins, however, suggest a rather swashbuckling tone that I had overlooked. It was founded in 1948 by three families including my own – the Watkinses (my grandfather), the Whitemans and the Davieses. The name derived from the Desert Rats, the 7th Armoured Division that fought in major battles in North Africa, and later in Italy and north-west Europe, during the Second World War. They had a reputation as a rather *ad hoc* bunch, moving in quickly and effectively from behind enemy lines, hitting their target and getting out again as fast as possible. And this too is the essence of the shoot. It is like no other.

We met at the Davies's home, Bucknell House, with the usual meet and greet although it was a trip down memory lane for me. Our host, Will Davies, is the third generation of 'Rats' and an old friend whom I hadn't seen for a long time. His sister, Lou, and I used to meet on our ponies and ride for hours as children. Will was always tinkering with an airgun and delighted in shooting something just as we mounted up, startling the horses and sending us bolting down the drive. All these stories, and more, had a good airing as we reminisced.

Before we all climbed into 4x4s there was a little welcoming speech and the presentation of a beautiful crystal bowl to me, because I was the first duchess to join the shoot for a day! There was also an award for Will's son, Jamie, for recently shooting his first teal. Many nods and winks were aimed at my absent brother, William, who was running a shoot at Heartsease on the same day – and, of course, nobody wanted to 'pinch' his birds... I had forgotten how much this team of old friends enjoyed teasing each other, and everyone else, and the whole day was one mickey-take after another. 'Let's go ratting!' someone called out exuberantly and that was that – the day was officially under way.

I jumped into Will's vehicle and we had a great time talking about the old days and how the shoot works now. All the Guns are great mates and pay £400

a season which covers the cost of putting 500 pheasants down to shoot over eight days. Peter Hood (who kindly showed me round Brecon Moor for our Grouse chapter), was here, as was Peter McCutcheon, a retired bank manager, Nigel Cremer, John Bright, local farmer Geoff Fowden, who runs the local cattle market in Knighton, and James Middleton, known as Masher because he's not bothered how high the birds are as long as he kills them. We passed several landmarks from my childhood, the school, the chapel where I sang my first solo and the house where, legend has it, the local doctor was killed by a disgruntled patient and Will always used to play Black Sabbath on his car's music system whenever we went past.

As we pulled in at the first drive I heard the story about my father's initiation when he first joined as a Rat, a very long time ago. He was driven to a drive on the bonnet of a Land Rover and as they pulled in to stop, four pheasants were recklessly blasted to death on the roadside by someone shooting from the back of the vehicle. (Hideous – and I would like to think that no one would ever do something like that nowadays.) Apparently it was all designed to test his nerve – and he passed. Ironically, as Will recounted this tale, four pheasants happened to fly in front of us but all four got away. Another story involved the motor racing legend, Innes Ireland, who lived in Radnor and shot with the Rats on several occasions. He invited Peter Davies, Will's father, to Monaco to watch a Grand Prix in the sixties and during a visit to the pits at the beginning of the race, said to Peter: 'Not even this beats a day with the Rat Patrol.' Such a build-up!

I detected a slight hint of panic from Will as he reminded me that a big day here was fifty birds. But it is the fun, the skill and the banter that makes a day so special, not the numbers in the bag. Certainly there was no shortage of the former.

Slotted between Stanage and the Plowden Estate shoot I was surprised that the scrubby bit of land we were standing on next to a tiny wood could produce anything at all. My opinions have been proved wrong countless times writing this book, and were about to be so again – spectacularly. Like lightning, the Guns and beaters all found their places and within three minutes birds just kept appearing, seemingly out of nowhere, high birds at that and unbelievably sporting. Will shot everything that came his way. Masher mashed his share and Geoff was ragged mercilessly for missing everything

*Wise advice from a senior rat.*

*Past and present rats unite.*

*Lunch with the rats.*

*The rats in retreat.*

*Below*
*The infamous Rat Patrol lining up with the day's bag laid out in front of Guns, beaters and pickers-up.*

You need thick skin on this shoot. The whole drive took about ten minutes by which time we were all back on the road to the next one.

The beaters were like laughing hyenas screaming over the hills at full pelt on the next drive, flapping their flags like men possessed. I felt the full force of the 'ratting experience' again and it was so good to be out. Geoff, sadly, failed again to hit much and continued to be mobbed for his nine-shots-to-one-bird ratio. The shoot's motto is rather grand: *nil expectare sic omnia bonus est*, meaning, expect nothing, thus anything is a bonus. It is certainly apt.

Mum joined us for lunch, which consisted of everyone's picnics pooled together and included chicken legs, Colston Bassett Stilton, pork pies, and various homemade flavoured gins. There was a sweepstake but, not surprisingly on this shoot, you didn't have to guess the number of birds in the bag but the number of legs. Someone, who shall remain nameless, wrote down an odd number!

The day continued as it had started and after lunch I joined the beaters. One of the drives was over a railway line and we all had to wait for the train from Bucknell to Shrewsbury before we could start. The wait, for me, conjured up images of a high-speed train or a long, snaking haulage affair, rattling along to its destination. When it eventually came, it was a tiddly little one carriage commuter train but still our excitement was huge as it signalled the start of the next drive. In true Rat Patrol form, it was over almost before it had begun.

At the end of a thrilling day a more than acceptable 136 legs had been counted in the bag: 66 pheasants and 2 pigeons. Well done, Mum! But the secret is out: she won the sweepstake with a guess of 135… The Rat Patrol was my last day of research and to be honest, of all the shoots I have been fortunate and privileged enough to visit, the best fun. Why? Because it doesn't matter how smart the venue, how big the bag and how high the birds, nothing beats a day with old friends doing what everyone loves most – shooting.

*Left*
*Nigel Cremer, one of the Ratters,*
*gathering the kill from the first drive.*

# PHIL BURTT'S TOP TIPS FOR PHEASANT SHOOTING

Pheasants are the starter game bird; everyone should learn to shoot winged game on a pheasant shoot – it's a tradition and a rite of passage for every Gun.

The best thing to do is to study the quality of the pheasant on the day. Sometimes you will shoot them over rides, which aren't always very challenging. If you shoot them on very flat ground they could be really wild and go everywhere, twisting and turning and make challenging shots. The quality high pheasant shooting in the West Country or Devon, Cornwall, Wales and Yorkshire, where birds can be really high is the most difficult: from very high to entirely out of gunshot range.

It doesn't matter if a pheasant is 20 yards or 120 yards into the sky; every bird properly presented to the Gun is a challenging shot.

Have the right ammunition. High bird days will require a heavier cartridge and probably a heavily choked gun. Over-and-unders are becoming popular for high birds but the choice is a personal preference.

Judge the quality of the bird on the day and do not let the host or keeper down by just picking the high birds. Every pheasant you are shown, high, medium or low should be honoured equally.

# 6
# WILD DUCK & GEESE

DUCK & GOOSE SHOOTING SEASON
1 SEPTEMBER – 31 JANUARY OR 20 FEBRUARY
IN ENGLAND AND WALES.
IF SHOOTING THE AREA OF SEASHORE
BELOW THE HIGH-WATER MARK

*The magical twilight hour before the duck flight on Salthouse marshes with Brent Pope.*

If ever an invitation was perfectly timed, this was it! After two consecutive nights of teenage parties at the castle (the Junior Belvoir Hunt Ball and our eldest daughter, Violet's, eighteenth), I was more than ready for a breather. A last-minute call to go duck flighting on Salthouse Marshes in north Norfolk answered all my prayers. Great friend Hannah Steiger-White, who is one of our photographers, and I jumped in the car to head for the east coast, leaving all the hormones and overtired kids behind. This was my first experience of duck flighting. Actually no, I tell a lie, my second.

My first was on 5 September 1980. I had just turned seventeen and I was with my father, his friend, Roger Deacon, and my brother William. We were waiting at a duck pool called The Big Foice in the hills at the back of the Forest Inn pub at Llanfihangel, about three miles from New Radnor. We were with another of Dad's mates, John Cutler, who farmed the land. Dusk descended and ducks started filling the sky. Guns were firing away. Four mallard were shot and one teal. Suddenly the neighbouring farmer and his son popped into view, scrambling out of the reeds where they had been hiding, having narrowly avoided being blown to pieces. My poor father was in such a state. I don't know what upset him more, nearly killing someone or discovering poachers – for he had seen these two selling game in the market earlier in the week. Suitable libations at the Forest Inn calmed him eventually, but the memory of the incident stayed with us all for ever.

# ON THE NORTH NORFOLK MARSHES

This second trip was very different. Proper wildfowling on marshes is about as far removed from shooting over a well-fed duck pond as you can get. We arrived in Norfolk on a beautiful sunny afternoon on 1 September and went to meet our host, Brent Pope, a very sprightly septuagenarian, and his wife, Brigid, at their home in Blakeney, just a few miles from Salthouse. Small world that we live in, one of the friends who had come to shoot with Brent was John Wainwright from Welshpool and we had many mutual friends from home.

Brent was keen to show me a scrapbook with a cutting about the actress, Keira Knightley. 'Don't think you're the first duchess on these marshes,' he tells

me. 'She was here filming *The Duchess* and we earned a handsome fee which we ploughed into the shoot's management account.' Another famous connection, in the next village, is singer James Blunt, whose family used to own the windmill at Cley next the Sea – though the name is a bit of an anachronism, since land reclamation in the seventeenth century put some distance between Cley and the beach.

So, it's the first day of the season and at 5pm we set off in Brent's 4x4 to have a good look round. Brent's family has owned this 134-acre marsh since 1924 and he talked passionately about how he mows the rides around ponds and protects the natural environment just like his father had. Brent himself used to cut the reeds with part-time keeper Geoffrey Crowe until a few years ago. But he says they both got too old for the heavy manual labour and as part of his twenty-year Management Agreement with Natural England, local professional reed cutters now cut for him. Preserving habitats for wildlife are part of the deal too, so a percentage of the reeds is always left standing to provide breeding and nesting habitats for sedge, bearded tits, reed and grasshopper warblers, as well as very rare but increasingly sighted bittern and marsh harriers.

Reed cutting for thatch has been an essential industry on the marshes for centuries, traditionally generating income for local people in winter. During the 1990s cheaper foreign imports threatened local employment but the North Norfolk Reed Cutters' Association, formed in 2004, united with all the other marsh associations to restore and expand the local market, which has proved a great success.

The ephemeral marsh landscape has certainly seen much change over the decades and as a consequence wildfowling has changed too. The days of shooting anything and everything with wings are long gone. Since the Wildlife and Countryside Act of 1981 more and more species are protected to give some of our rarest birds a chance to survive and thrive. There is still plenty to satisfy the wildfowler though and the British Association for Shooting and Conservation (BASC) Wildfowlers' Code of Conduct keeps all shooters abreast of the latest developments and sets out stringent guidelines. Like all game shooting, everything boils down to the same mantra: respect for your quarry.

*Taking a break
from shooting to make notes
for the book.*

# BRENT POPE'S TOP TIPS FOR DEVELOPING A WILD DUCK POND

You need a good supply of water to enable you either to flood an area of marsh or grassland or dig out a flight pond with a water depth of, ideally, two to three inches, which is perfect for feeding.

It is relatively easy to flood grassland because land is uneven and will give plenty of shallow areas which are crucial for feeding and for natural food to survive such as worms etc.

A dug-out flight pond with banked-up sides could be too deep, so you will need

a lower ditch to enable you to drop the water level in places.

Ideally, dig a pond that allows a constant supply of fresh water to run through it.

I like to dry out my ponds and flooded areas for the summer so I can get machinery in for maintenance.

Reed can spread six feet a year so remember to spray it off or it will choke your pond. I use Roundup when the plant is in full leaf but this must not be

done over water. There are very strict guidelines about spraying near water, so be careful.

For food I use barley mostly, although some people use wheat, especially for teal. I feed every day by hand, spreading the corn as widely as possibly. Don't chuck a whole bucketful in one place. The more you spread the food the more duck will be attracted. Teal and mallard in particular do not like to feed too close together. Teal tend to tear about and unsettle the mallard, which is why one

pond might attract mostly mallard and another, teal.

Some people feed old potatoes but watch you don't encourage rats if you do. Rat pee can turn the water sour very quickly.

Once you have started feeding, keep disturbances down to a minimum. When the duck start to arrive, stand at a safe distance and watch – or shoot.

This part of our coastline is of enormous interest on a global scale and there is no shortage of environmentalists blazing a trail for progress. The Intergovernmental Panel on Climate Change regularly publishes assessment reports that require legislation and guidance to continue investigating the impact of climate change on the environment. Meaning? Continual changes being required in the management of privately owned marshes.

It makes no difference whether people believe it is the will of nature and its cyclical behavioural pattern, not global warming, that causes the problems: whatever the cause, increased flooding, which destroys sea defences and swamps marshland causing higher salinity levels in ponds, is so detrimental to the survival of some species. Either way, government bodies have stepped up their conservation programmes and produced a set of guidelines for landowners delineating how best to preserve the habitat. For Brent this means, he hopes, entry to Natural England's Higher Level Stewardship scheme and funding to continue maintaining the marsh habitats to conserve their wildlife. What does this mean for wildfowlers? Big Brother watching very closely to ensure that nothing jeopardises the scheme's objectives.

Politics aside, Mossy, Brent's black labrador (aka Black Bastard or Black Billy) twitches with excitement in the back of the car. We drive over the marsh as Brent explains the migration and how these extraordinary birds start their epic journeys from Russia, Scandinavia and Scotland on the Eastern Flyway, some to winter by the shingle beach, saline lagoons and reedbeds whilst the majority carry on as far as the Camargue in the South of France. It's the same year after year with pinkfooted geese usually first on the scene. One exception came after the 1986 Chernobyl disaster when only a quarter of the normal wigeon population returned.

On a more cheerful note he shows me where some starlet sea anemones have recently been found in saline ponds – they were feared lost after the storm surge in November 2007. There are only a few coastal lagoons in the UK where this Red List endangered species can be found so the anemones' presence is of huge significance and very illustrative of the work of all these organisations. We also see plenty of fresh water ponds which Brent has built over the years and that he feeds. One of them, Duke's Pond, is named after the Duke of Edinburgh, who was a guest here when his friend, Lord Buxton, rented the shoot. Today Brent runs a syndicate of local farmers and businessmen and

*Mallard, which Brent Pope's wife Brigid probably knows more ways to cook than anyone I know.*

*Above*
*Brent Pope (second from left) at*
*Salthouse Marshes with Paddy,*
*the keeper, kneeling in front.*

they shoot about once a week throughout the season.

As twilight falls we gather together and the Guns draw peg numbers. Brent sends them off to the island stands. The sun sets and the light peters out with a darkening orange glow; everything looks promising to me but Brent's worried that it might not be a good night for flighting. Ideally you need a good northeasterly wind but there is only a gentle breeze. He and Paddy stand back: they are not shooting, preferring to watch. Fortunately the wind picks up a bit and the sound of a single distant duck or goose crescendoes into a deafening commotion. More and more ducks fill the sky, banking above while they pick their place for landing. Brent can identify a breed from an incredible distance and pointed out various birds that were coming in but it isn't easy to spot them as they

are silhouetted against the darkening sky: it takes experience. Then the guns started firing. Each shot was clicked on a counting machine and each bird was marked for retrieving.

We were out for about three hours and when Brent was happy that a fair number of birds had been shot he blew the hooter to stop. I was fascinated to see how the gundogs picked their birds in the dark with just the light from the Guns' torches and their good noses to direct them. Later in the year it will be easier for them to work after the leaves have fallen. Small teal can get lodged in thick green reed and don't always fall through to the ground, making it difficult to retrieve them. Mossy, however, has an amazing nose and missed nothing. When everyone was sure that all the birds had been picked they were taken to Brent's marsh shed and counted. Teal and mallard hung on nails for collection while we drank a warming glass of sloe gin to beat off the cool night chill.

The talk was of the birds that had got away and who had shot particularly well. I chatted to Paddy, who had been a bait-digger, bricklayer and general maintenance man at the nearby Blakeney Hotel. The marsh is his second home. He tells me there isn't a corner of it he doesn't know and love. Both his sons and daughter have moved away from the area and I can't help feeling a little sad that there will be no more Paddys to enthuse over and share all his incredible knowledge. However Brent's son and daughter will one day take over from him. They were both named after duck – Ferina after a pochard and Laysan after teal from the Laysan Island in the Pacific – and have been indoctrinated since birth into the ways of ducks and the importance of looking after the marsh. Their names certainly won't allow them to forget their heritage. I suppose you can only get away with naming your children like that when you yourself have been named Brent after a goose…

By 9.30pm I was thinking it must be nearly time to leave and head back for supper when a car rolled up. It was the butcher from P & S Butchers in nearby Holt; he'd arrived to collect his share of game. He is a countryman and his wife is learning to shoot. He told me he had firm orders for wild duck and that he would have them plucked and dressed by morning! There is a minimal carbon footprint in that transaction: self-sufficiency at its most efficient. Can there be a better way?

We returned to the Popes' house for Brigid's supper, not duck as I'd anticipated but a free-range chicken from the local butcher with vegetables from the garden. Another reminder that today's buzz-words, biodiversity, sustainability and food miles, are nothing new.

This trip had been a learning curve in every sense: first, I had been introduced properly to wildfowling and second, I was beginning to understand about the bureaucracy that can sometimes overshadow the good work and intentions of a small shoot. This part of the north Norfolk coast is one of the key conservation sites in Europe and the Blakeney and District Wildfowlers' Association, formed in 1927, was one of the first members of The Wildfowlers' Association of Great Britain and Ireland, WAGBI. The parent organisation changed its named in 1981 to British Association

for Shooting and Conservation (BASC) and in 2004 joined forces with English Nature, now called Natural England. The Norfolk Coast Partnership works with all the stakeholders. The Norfolk Wildlife Trust manages Salthouse Marsh, which is also an Area of Outstanding Natural Beauty, a Ramsar site, a Biosphere Reserve, a Site of Special Scientific Interest, a Special Protection Area and a candidate for Special Area for Conservation and a Marine Special Area of Conservation. I'm sure I've forgotten someone but the point is, Brent is finding it increasingly difficult to do anything without treading on someone's toes.

As an outsider, having witnessed the incredible ecosystem and wildlife on this extraordinary stretch of our coastline in a visit of less than five hours, I'm very grateful to Brent – and wildfowling – for the opportunity to experience such intense conservation at first hand.

# GOOSE SHOOTING IN CAITHNESS

Having had a fabulous introduction to wildfowling on the north Norfolk coast I was ready to see a goose flight. I had met someone called Toby Ward during a family fishing and stalking holiday in Sutherland, Scotland. Toby, and Patrick Hungerford, own Bighouse Lodge where we stayed, which has fishing rights on the River Halladale, a spate salmon river. They let it out for several weeks a year, offering fishing, stalking, driven partridge and pheasant, walked-up grouse over dogs, wildfowling for geese and duck, woodcock and snipe to help with the running costs. Funnily enough, Brent Pope stays here for holidays too.

It is worth mentioning that the estate has a crofting community. I remember, prior to the Reform Act in 2003, which gave crofters the right to buy their crofts, how nervous some landowners had been about the potential implications of changes in ownership but at Bighouse all efforts are made to ensure relationships between the estate and crofters work harmoniously.

Toby had promised he'd take me goose flighting and so at the beginning of October, we headed north again. I stayed at Bighouse Lodge again, only this time as a guest of Toby and Patrick, which is an experience in itself as these two hospitable hosts wine, dine and entertain like no others. Visitors are asked to bring fruit and vegetables as gifts and in return you are sent home

*Above*
*A quick chat with Paddy before the flight.*

with a boot full of game and fish so it's a fair trade and they cook the most delicious food. Everything they eat is local because it has to be, but is no less varied for that. Dinner was a very jolly affair. One of of Toby's sons was there with friends for stalking and as we talked about our forthcoming goose expedition, Patrick and Toby both launched into their hilarious impressions of geese coming in to land. Arms flap and lots of honking goose noises are made. The younger generation had obviously seen it all before and barely seem to notice as the acting became more and more animated. Patrick seats himself at the piano and plays all sorts of suitably dramatic music as Toby continues with his description and demonstration of geese coming over in a V-formation. The performers compare the noise of the birds' approach to sitting in the stalls at the Albert Hall listening to a soprano soloist getting louder and louder, until a full chorus reaches fortissimo from forte. The two of them could easily double as Hinge and Bracket.

In readiness for our big day Toby called Pattie Wilson, a nearby crofter and highly respected wildfowling and goose-flighting guide, who lives forty minutes from Bighouse in Caithness. We are hoping to see wild greylag geese migrating from Iceland and we will need to leave at 5am to be in position for first light at about 6am. But, returning to the room with telephone in hand, Toby declares that there are no geese. 'What!' I shriek. Look, I know and understand about the vagaries of pitching a sport against the wiles of nature. How many times have we heard of people coming back from a week's fishing trip where there were no fish, or disappointed from a shoot when the weather was too mild, foggy or snowed off – but to travel ten hours to the most northerly point of the British Isles to hear that there were no geese was humbling to say the least. Perhaps it was a necessary reminder that nothing about this sport of shooting is ever guaranteed. But the phrase 'wild goose chase' did inevitably spring to mind.

I'd bought a fabulously unattractive khaki-coloured ski-suit to camouflage myself and keep warm and, having come all this way, I was still anxious to see what might have been, with or without geese. Toby sighed with relief and we agreed to leave at 8.30am the following morning – but he made me promise not to wear the said ski-suit. No comment.

*Left*
*All the goose decoys positioned*
*but alas not a real one in sight,*
*just starlings.*

*Right*
*With Pattie Wilson, the gooseflighting*
*guide from Caithness,*
*on the way back from a no-show!*

After a hearty breakfast of kippers and coffee we set off for Caithness. Just before arriving there we pulled over. Toby had spotted a formation of geese flying over us but they weren't heading for our destination, sadly. We meet Pattie, a wonderfully cheerful sheep and cattle farmer, who loves wildfowling and happily admits to an obsession with geese. He gave me some fascinating insights into the life of a crofter too and how their opportunities have changed since 2003. He has been able to buy his croft on the Watten Estate in Caithness with 120 acres of mixed grass and rough pasture and recently purchased another 180 acres which, together with land he rents from the estate, enables him and his son to run a sustainable family business. It is so reassuring for the future of these sparsely populated areas to see two generations working the same land. As well as farming Pattie indulges his passion for shooting and takes clients both wildfowling and goose flighting, which observes its own set of rules and regulations. You can check the BASC website for all the legal restrictions. I was interested to learn that unlike duck shooting you cannot feed geese but you can use decoys in their feeding grounds in the morning. There is a bag limit of five pinkfeet or two greylag geese per Gun per day and it is illegal to sell wild geese. You will never see wild goose on a menu, which makes eating one you've shot yourself rather special.

Pattie has no shortage of shooting stories but his eyes really sparkle when he recalls seeing 10,000 geese flying off a loch at night in the familiar V-formation which stretched over nearly three miles. As well as greylag there are pinkfeet, Egyptian and Canada geese that fly at 20 to 30 miles an hour over a 600-mile distance from Iceland. When they get to the Caithness shoreline they are exhausted.

So here we are, albeit without geese to shoot. Ironically, thirty metres from the ridge we are standing on, we see a field of greylag geese tucking into the crop. Toby takes me to where we would have 'hidden' in order to shoot them – in a ditch. Because you could be lying in one position for a long time while you're waiting you need to be warm and dry, hence my purchase of the dreaded ski-suit. A little later Pattie demonstrates his goose-calling technique with a short reed goose call but it's more than just blowing into a whistle: it's an incredible art to time the calls correctly as you listen to the geese honking above. We all had a go, but still no geese for us.

Despite the disappointment I had loved every minute of my trip. I thanked Pattie for his time and patience and said goodbye. All I had to do now was find some geese to shoot and preferably nearer to home.

# GOOSE SHOOTING AT BELVOIR

The expression 'can't see for looking' sprang to mind when we picked our final destination to shoot this elusive quarry. The lakes at Belvoir are of course under our noses but the lure of the wilds of northern Scotland was too strong to resist and so different from home. Here we are though, this time with the boys, Charles and Hugo, ready to see what goose flighting is all about.

A goose will eat about the same amount as a sheep and with about a thousand Canada and greylag skeins arriving every winter to munch through our oil seed rape, wheat and barley, that's a lot of damage. On top of that, probably because of some recent sub-zero winter temperatures, they don't all move off in the spring any more either. So the boys were delighted when I suggested that they might like to have a go at shooting some. They set off one afternoon with Clive Tinkler, who takes them ferreting every Sunday, to build a hide for a 5am goose-flighting session the following morning with Phil Burtt.

Both boys have done a bit of driven shooting: Charles with his 20-bore and Hugo with a .410. They were genuinely very excited about tackling a completely different quarry. So with everything ready for the following day they were happy to have an early night whilst I organised the breakfast picnic and plenty of warm clothes. The air was rather crisp at that time of the morning in late October and as we made our way to meet Phil on the bridge there was no sign of dawn. We settled ourselves in the hide with hot chocolate, guns out of sleeves, and waited. Within about quarter of an hour the boys, already beginning to squabble, were silenced by the start of the dawn chorus. We sat totally mesmerised by this most magical part of the day as it gradually unveiled to the sound of songbirds, with bunnies scampering about looking for breakfast and cock pheasants strutting and ruffling their feathers, all under the magnificent breaking night sky.

*Above*
*Pattie Wilson - a devoted wild fowler.*

*Above*
*On the front steps at Bighouse*
*with Patrick Hungerford (left) and*
*Toby Ward (right).*

*Right*

*Charles making contact with his*

*first goose in full view of his*

*proud Mum as it crumples in the sky.*

But an hour and a half passed and still no geese had appeared; the boys were bickering again. They also baited me about my optimism and reminded me that I had thought I was going to see geese in Caithness – what did I know? But just as I was losing any shred of respect from my sons, Phil heard a distant honk. That got their attention, you could even hear them breathing! Twenty minutes later, though, still nothing, and just as we were preparing to accept defeat a quiet but definite sound alerted us, growing louder and louder as literally hundreds of geese made their way towards the lake. I have never seen Charles and Hugo so excited in all my life.

Hundreds and hundreds of geese stretched out across the eerie, sepia-coloured sky in their striking V-formation and – joy of unbelievable joys – appeared to be heading for our decoys. We didn't have a goose-caller like the one Pattie Wilson uses in Caithness, but Phil cupped his hands together and gave some sort of impersonation, enough for the boys to collapse into giggles anyway, but it seemed to work.

Hugo, determined to match anything his brother might achieve, despite the four-year age gap, quietly eyes up the scene, pulls his gun into his shoulder and tucks his head on his stock, eyes fixed on his Concorde-like target; and this calm eight-year-old boy pulls the trigger. Apparently without any fear that he could possibly miss, he shot his first goose stone dead. Alton Towers eat your heart out: nothing could match this for thrills. Charles followed with equal success and that was that; the dawning of a new obsession that left poor Phil at the mercy of early alarm-calls to take the boys goose flighting for the rest of halfterm. But it wasn't just the shooting that excited them; what surprised me more than anything was that they actually loved being up so early and experiencing all that Mother Nature has to offer at such an early hour. I realised, as the days passed, that they were seeing the countryside from a different perspective. Yes, we live in a beautiful Capability Brown parkland setting and yes, we have lots of opportunities to enjoy it – but they were beginning to grow into countrymen, and I was very proud of them.

*Clive Tinkler teaches*
*Charles and Hugo*
*the art of goose decoying.*

# PATTIE WILSON'S TOP TIPS FOR SHOOTING GEESE & DUCKS

### SHOOTING GEESE

Check the field the day before you intend to shoot just to ensure they haven't moved off.

Wear good camouflage gear with hat and face veil.

Always use top quality cartridges

Set up decoy geese with the farthest away decoy about 25 metres from your hide – decoys should be placed so geese fly towards them.

If geese don't respond to the decoys in the first four or five skeins, give up as it's not going to work. Try again another day.

### SHOOTING DUCKS

Feed your pond at least twice a week but don't overfeed.

Don't over-shoot – leave before the stragglers come in.

Avoid shooting when the moon is up as ducks are unlikely to come in.

Ensure you have a good gundog that will retrieve everything to avoid missing wounded ducks.

Use a dozen or so decoys if possible to entice them in, or a duck-call or wigeon whistle.

# 7

# SNIPE & WOODCOCK

WOODCOCK SHOOTING SEASON
IN ENGLAND, WALES,
NORTHERN IRELAND & THE ISLE OF MAN
1 OCTOBER – 31 JANUARY

IN SCOTLAND
1 SEPTEMBER – 31 JANUARY

COMMON SNIPE SHOOTING SEASON
12 AUGUST – 31 JANUARY

*Feeling very bedraggled but
what a day!*

# THE ISLE OF MUCK

When Heather McGregor brought Emma Weir to stay for a partridge shoot at Belvoir, I was very lucky that Emma offered to introduce me to driven snipe shooting with partridge, pheasant, duck, geese and woodcock on the Isle of Muck. After our fun but fruitless visit to Caithness for geese we left for Arisaig, on the west coast of Scotland, before boarding the ferry to Muck to find some snipe.

Emma runs a successful global executive search firm in London and bought Arisaig House in 2010. As a child she had holidayed close by in Moidart and like all of us, probably, had romantic thoughts of returning and reliving a misspent youth. This time she was going to shoot too. When she and I were children, girls were not encouraged to pick up a gun, but now she was determined to do things her way. Accompanied by her beloved sprocker (springer crossed with cocker), with a Beretta 14½-inch stock, 26-inch barrel, over-and-under 20-bore shotgun in her hand and some shooting lessons behind her, she is making a good start.

Her sister and brother-in-law, Peter and Sarah Winnington-Ingram, run the house – once the HQ of the Special Operations Executive during the Second World War – and offer bed-and-breakfast, which was perfect for our party of snipe shooters. The house's website describes the last leg of the journey thus: '… taking the fabled Road to the Isles from Fort William through the hills and by glittering lochs. You pass historic landing places recalling the early triumphs and final tragedy of Bonnie Prince Charlie, to arrive at what must be most people's ultimate idea of a romantic hideaway… an honest grey stone mansion, originally built in 1864…' The description doesn't disappoint. It is a truly magnificent setting with views towards Muck, the tiny island that is only about two miles long and one mile wide with a population of thirty-seven.

Romance was in the air too as Emma had invited a new man in her life to join the party. Everyone was keen to meet the poor chap who I feared was about to be subjected to a real inquisition. But we'll have to wait as he won't be arriving until tomorrow. Another guest in the party was Lucilla Noble, whom I had met on the same night as I met my husband at a dinner party in London. Her late husband, Sir Iain, was involved in all sorts of Scottish enterprises including

producing whisky and owning the Hotel Eilean Iarmain in the south of Skye that also hosts shooting parties.

After an excellent dinner, I headed off to bed and set my alarm so that I could watch Wales play Ireland in the quarter-finals of the Rugby World Cup first thing in the morning, a match which turned out to be well worth the early start. Wales's victory seemed like the perfect omen for my first snipe shoot. As we all head off for the jetty to pick up the ferry from Arisaig to Port Mor we meet the 'new man', who is extremely nice and mercifully not mobbed. We boarded the boat and I popped into the cab to sit with ferryman Ronnie Dyer, who showed me photographs of all the marine life he has seen during crossings. There are minke whales, basking sharks and dolphins. Will we see any today, I ask? 'Maybe, maybe,' is as good an answer as I'm going to get and I'm starting to think this sounds as optimistic as the prospects of seeing greylag geese in Caithness. My good omen for seeing snipe is feeling a bit jaded already.

In the summer, Ronnie ferries over 300 passengers a day from Muck to Arisaig and also transports food and supplies. In winter the tourists are obviously few and far between so the presence of shooting parties helps the local economy in an otherwise lean period. If the weather had been clear we would have seen Eigg but not today as the cloud and drizzle is relentless.

It is pouring with rain by the time we dock but we are met by a shirtsleeved Toby Fichtner-Irvine who runs the small-scale family shoot that stretches over most of the island. First things first, we call into the island's Visitor Centre where we are served bacon rolls and steaming hot coffee. This is a family shoot where literally all the family are involved. The McEwan family own the island and the Port Mor Hotel and Mr McEwan's daughter, Mary, is married to Toby, who does the cooking with Mary's mother, Jenny. Son Alexander, aged eight, hands round the goodies and a nip of sloe gin and when we've listened to the instructions for our day he points to his school and describes his six classmates to us.

Toby lets about ten days of mixed drives of pheasant and partridges during the season, with later on plenty of woodcock and snipe too which is the big pull for which clients will travel far and wide. Unbelievably there are no predators on the island, which accounts for the very healthy eighty per cent return of the birds

*Home brews from the island. Strawberry vodka*

*Rough crossing on the ferry to the Isle of Muck.*

*Taking aim.*

vegetables in polytunnels and supplies all the islanders. As he throws the birds on to the rails he adds, 'we all multi-task here you know', bearing out what I had already been told. Dave wasn't born on the island but assures me he'd never leave. Toby tells us about the simple straightforward community life on Muck: everyone is valued and everyone has a place.

On to the next drive and the promise of snipe. I'm standing on a steep hill with ponds and the sea below, mist and light rain in my face and a new loader, Emma's new man, with me when… oh my… snipe! Darting about all over the place, flitting from side to side at incredible speed. Yes, I've been told only a few pellets will kill one but please, I hadn't even got the gun mounted. And again… a possible left and right. Everyone is screaming up the line to me, 'Emma – snipe'! I try to hand the gun to my loader to give someone a chance of hitting one but alas, as quickly as they come, they go. All those missed opportunities to bag my first snipe – gone. Returning to the 4x4, I feel like a cricketer who has just been bowled out for a duck, taking the long walk back to the pavilion. But what an amazing sight they were!

Lunch at the Visitor Centre was as good as you would get in a top organic London restaurant. Tender flakes of Old Spot boar minced pork, cooked with cumin and apples, in a shortcrust pastry pie with apple gravy, was absolute perfection. We were in the only building on the island that had power too that day as the wind turbine had broken so electricity was only available at night. I met Dave's wife who runs the island's shop, The Green Shed, which is stocked with provisions and local crafts. As I said, shooting extends the tourist season for everyone on the island.

A combination of a superb lunch and adrenalin started everyone singing on the way to the next drive. Though the rain had really set in, Toby was still in his shirtsleeves and everyone was happy – it seemed like a good time to celebrate. The only misfortune was zero snipe on the record card but that was my fault.

On the way back to the ferry at the end of the day we called in to The Green Shed and I bought a beautiful felt bowl (made by Dave's wife) for Emma, who had been such a perfect host. We were waved off by three generations of the McEwan family and I too longed to be with my family. They would have loved all this.

that he puts down. The panoramic views of deep gullies and heather banks, the twenty acres of new game crops that have been planted beside new and existing plantations, with the sea as a backdrop, are truly magnificent.

So, the first drive. Emma is expecting me to shoot and won't take any hesitation, never mind no, from me. So here we go, nerves and all. I tuck the stock tight into my chin, the safety catch is off and I ignore the rain and the mild nervous shakes. Pheasants and partridges suddenly appear in waves. I take aim, fire and hurray, knock one dead. My good omen from the Welsh win is paying dividends after all.

On our way to the second drive we have to wait for three wild hill ponies to move off the road. They are used to bring stags off the hill from stalking parties and the family breeds them to sell. While we were waiting I chatted to Alexander McEwan, Mary's father, who at the age of seventy has handed over the reins of the estate to his children. He is as fit as a man half his age. I had spotted Alexander, his grandson, struggling to keep up with him earlier. He tells me how the whole population has to multi-task and though newcomers are welcomed they don't all fit in and many leave.

By the second drive I'm more relaxed and am very pleased to shoot four more birds, though there are no snipe. But as we walk back to the 4x4 out of nowhere one suddenly appears ahead, then two more. Maybe we'll be in luck after all. We finish our elevenses of strawberry, raspberry and sloe gin and vodka from pewter mugs and polish off some homemade pork pies and brownies. Everything we eat is from the island. Toby introduces me to Dave Barnden, who is loading birds into the game cart, and he explains how he grows

*Gathering for a team photo in front of the Visitor Center. A warm retreat for lunch.*

# THE ARUNDELL ARMS AT LIFTON

I still wanted to shoot a snipe or at least see someone else shoot one, but fate still seemed to be against me. I had heard that driven snipe shooting was pioneered in the 1930s at the Arundell Arms hotel at Lifton on the Devon-Cornwall border and I hoped to join a party on my way to a pheasant shoot in Cornwall but sadly it didn't work out. Instead the owner, Adam Fox-Edward, very kindly explained the hotel's history to me.

The Fox-Edward family has owned this lovely hotel for fifty years and boasts that guests can participate in a country sporting activity every day of the year whether it be fishing for salmon or trout, shooting, or hunting with nearby packs of hounds. The hotel's fishing courses are legendary too but it is the snipe I'm interested in.

Snipe shooting has indeed been a speciality since the 1930s, when the hotel was owned and run by the Morris family. They owned the Ambrosia factory in the village too and bought all the milk from local farmers who were happy to grant permission for the family and their guests to shoot over their land. After all, how could a farmer refuse when his monthly milk cheque was involved! It seems that few believed that people would pay to travel long distances to shoot such a small and difficult bird, and you can picture the reaction from locals when the first guests arrived.

In the early days, with virtually no cars on rural roads, Guns often stood in the middle of the highway. Beaters would start from behind a hedge at the far side of a field and move towards the Guns waving a flag, exactly as it is done today, only no one stands in the road any more with a loaded shotgun. A whistle would be blown when the snipe flushed and the fun would begin. Guns had some very testing and enormously satisfying shooting at these small, fast, wild birds, which could come at any angle, height or speed. Prewar farming was rather different from today's intense agriculture, with smaller fields, little land drainage, and mostly organic manures. There must have been vast numbers of snipe. Records show bags of up to forty-eight in a day.

These hearty little birds are winter migrants, although a very small number nest high up on the moors during the summer. Arundell guests have shot

*Above*

*A successful day.*

at least three birds ringed in Gdansk, Poland, which shows the strong east-to-west movement of the Flyway as the continent freezes each autumn. They can be found over a wide range of land from the few marshes and rough moors still remaining to ploughed ground, maize stubbles, or grass pastures that have been well spread with slurry and left to stand over winter.

Today the hotel's guests still see a lot of snipe, with wisps of sometimes fifty or more over the Guns all at once. David Pilkington, Adam's fisheries manager and frequent beater, adds: 'I was privileged to be beating one chilly day a few years ago when we actually picked seventeen birds from a single drive. They were being flushed from a kale field, which was being strip-grazed

*Above*
*Standing on the front steps of*
*Adrian Bourke's home, Castlehill*
*at Ballina in County Mayo,*
*before venturing out for an afternoon's*
*woodcock shooting.*
*Bottom row from left, Adrian Bourke, me,*
*woodcock guru Peter Bacon,*
*and Peter's daughter, Hazel.*

and well poached up. The shot birds were falling behind the Guns into standing kale, and we probably failed to find all of them. They can be notoriously difficult to pick, although once your dog has acquired the nose for them he will easily trounce a highly bred and trained pheasant-finder.'

As a driven bird, the snipe ranks very highly. Evidently they are easily turned by anyone stupid enough to poke his head above the hedge to see what is coming. They fly upwards all the time when they are flushed and can reach quite a height after crossing larger fields. Guns have been known to say that they were out of shot but that is rarely the case; being so small they do not take a lot of killing, rather, they take some hitting! Apparently one party of Guns, with no experience of snipe, was a little amused to hear that the kill-to-cartridge ratio is normally around one to ten. David said the same party was less than amused when they had all fired (unsuccessfully) at a wisp, which had spread well along the line, when he asked them where he should send his dog to pick their birds!

David added: 'As a beater it is easy to see when a bird has been shot because the angle of the flight will change from upwards to downwards, but if a bird doesn't crumple and fall, the Gun may be unaware that the bird was hit. With a labrador at heel, it is always very satisfying to mark and pick that bird, and present it to the Gun.'

Snipe were to elude me for now but it was time to see some woodcock shooting and I had a fabulous trip planned to Ireland at the beginning of December.

# WOODCOCK SHOOTING IN THE WEST OF IRELAND

I had met Peter Bacon at the CLA Game Fair a number of years ago and he has visited us several times at Belvoir with a party of Irish shooters. He is well known in Ireland for his economic consultancy work for the Irish government but he is passionate about field sports and the countryside and is currently Chairman of the Countryside Alliance, Ireland. He very kindly invited me to the west of Ireland to sample some woodcock shooting.

*Right*
*Guns and beaters at*
*Temple House in County Sligo.*

I took an early morning flight from East Midlands airport to Knock International on Ireland's west coast, and by lunchtime I was at Castlehill at Ballina in County Mayo, home of Adrian Bourke (Mary Robinson's brother – she was formerly president of Ireland) for an afternoon's walked-up woodcock.

Castlehill is a small, private estate tucked beneath Mount Nephin, extending to the shores of Lough Conn – an 18,800-acre lake fed by the River Deel and drained by the River Moy. The Georgian house is every inch the Irish country gentleman's sporting lodge, built specifically for woodcock shooting and brown trout and salmon fishing on Lough Conn.

A quick lunch of soup and sandwiches gave me time to meet the rest of the team. Shoot organiser Michael Lennon has spent his career with the Irish Fisheries Protection Service and he brought along a couple of colleagues, Gerry Hoban and Conor

Dennedy. There was a definite fishy feel to the party with the presence of another fisheries manager, Granville Nesbitt of The Foxford Fishery on the renowned River Moy, which accounts for over thirty per cent of the annual rod catch of salmon in Ireland. Dr Joe Gilvarry, a medical practitioner and a passionate snipe and woodcock shot, joined us, with Declan Collins, a farmer and in-shore fisherman with a roguish eye – a real 'Flurry Knox' character straight out of Somerville and Ross's *The Irish RM*. Finally there was Hazel, Peter's gorgeous daughter, who was to be my companion for the next couple of days.

Michael Lennon called the Guns to attention in true brigadier style and at 1.30pm, along with an assortment of English springer and cocker spaniels, we set off on foot to hunt the strips (referred to as 'stripes') of cover which radiate from Castlehill to the shore of Lough Conn. Adrian waved us off from the steps

*Right*
*Gareth Norris (left),*
*Darrell Marshall (centre) with his*
*left-and-right, and Peter Bacon.*

outside his front door and, as I was to learn later, spent the afternoon preparing a wonderful dinner.

Three beating Guns – and dogs – progressed into the cover with two flanking Guns behind, at about fifty metres apart. We didn't have to wait long for action. Within five minutes there were several shouts of ''cock! 'cock! 'cock!' from Michael Lennon, who could be heard but not seen, from deep within the birch, willow and hazel scrub cover. Two shots rang out and everyone stopped while the dogs were sent to retrieve and then we all moved forward again.

Two birds rose on my side into a watery winter sky, one of which Peter dispatched with elegant ease while his wife's blue-roan cocker, Maisie, retrieved it with equal aplomb. By the time we got to the bottom of the stripe, we were standing knee-deep in floodwater from Lough Conn. But what with all the excitement and carrying six brace of woodcock in a game sling, it didn't seem to matter. Dr Joe, who had shot two and half brace himself, talked to me about the respect he holds for woodcock and how important it is to him that the precious habitat on which these migratory birds rely is preserved for the next generation.

Joe's young son James, aged ten, has just started shooting and is learning about fieldcraft from his father. One should not underestimate just how important these traditions are to this happy bunch of Guns. They are all drawn together from various social backgrounds by a common and deep love of the countryside and a knowledge and respect for every inch of the habitat where they hunt. Castlehill is private and as such is shot only twice, either side of Christmas. The rest of the time it is preserved and left undisturbed for the woodcock.

On we go to the next stripe and flush more of these 'elusive and crepuscular' birds, as Peter refers to them, but they are too numerous to count. By 4pm the

*Above*
*A pint of Guinness to finish the*
*day in Durkin's Pub, Ballinacarrow*
*in County Sligo.*

light was fading and the sun was setting in the west. A quick skirmish through the covers around the house yielded a few more and then it was back to the house. Dr Joe popped the cork from a welcome bottle of bubbly and the bag for the day was laid out. A grand, fourteen brace was the total for the afternoon, from in excess of about fifty brace flushed.

It was time to unwind before dinner and I made my way to where I was staying nearby at a very welcoming guesthouse, Enniscoe House, run by Susan Kellett and her family. Susan has plenty of people to stay in the winter for a couple of local woodcock syndicates and her home is popular in the summer too, with anglers fishing for salmon and trout on Lough Conn.

Dinner at Adrian's that evening represented Irish hospitality and craic at its best. Dr Joe's wife, Sam, and Michael's wife, Breege, joined the Guns while Adrian's daughter, Catherine, was our gracious hostess for the evening. Her father's afternoon in the kitchen had not been wasted. The rib of beef, from his organically reared herd of Dexter cattle, melted in the mouth it was so good. Dr Joe – dressed in a white coat for the occasion – did the honours with the carving knife and all the vegetables were from Adrian's kitchen garden. It was a perfect end to a perfect afternoon that left me with a memorable sense of the close-knit nature of these sporting friends who know and love their countryside, respect it and know how to enjoy life too.

We left Enniscoe the next morning in total darkness at 7.15am. A strong gale and lashing rain all night made for difficult driving for Hazel as the two of us followed closely behind Peter. It was an hour's drive to Temple House, in neighbouring County Sligo, the home of Roderick and Helena Perceval and a luxury guesthouse. The Perceval family has lived at Temple House since the seventeenth century and the estate has a long and distinguished history as a woodcock shoot, with records dating back to the 1880s. We were joining a party of Guns who had come from the UK for one of Roderick's three-day driven woodcock shooting packages. As well as the Temple House estate, Roderick holds extensive shooting rights by way of lease from Coillte, the Irish State Forestry Commission. He is able to shoot sixteen to twenty days a season without covering the same ground twice.

Our hosts were Mike and Penny Tanner, who have lived at Tavistock in Devon for many years, where Mike practises as a dentist and Penny is a psychotherapist.

They had already spent several days in October shooting snipe and had been coming to Temple House for a number of seasons. Driven woodcock shooting parties are an integral part of the Temple House visitor experience and there are plenty of shooting parties staying here during the winter.

We arrived just as the party were assembling for a fabulous breakfast in the house's very grand diningroom. The rain was easing as we set off to the first beat called Derreen, an extensive area of classical woodcock cover. We couldn't have asked for a better start as Darrell Marshall took a stunning left and right. Inclement weather, which had disturbed the birds overnight, could not dampen this party's sense of joy after that. There were three drives before lunch, in stunning wooded countryside, but the conditions were cold and difficult. The Irish take their shoot lunches no less seriously than the English and more veritable craic and a hearty venison casserole followed by a velvety, sticky toffee pudding kept us going through the afternoon. We continued for a further three drives before the weather really deteriorated and failing light finally got the upper hand. Seven and a half brace was a good outcome considering the conditions. We had flushed about twenty-four brace. Then it was off to Durkin's Pub in Ballinacarrow, where I had the pleasure of pulling my first pint of Guinness!

The following morning I left Temple House in snow and sleet, bound for Knock airport and home. How lucky I had been to enjoy a rare experience in the company of some wonderful characters. Long may these West of Ireland country house parties and their traditions continue.

Never having been on a woodcock or snipe shoot before writing this book, I finished my research wanting more. There is a magic about it that is so hard to explain. I would still love to see more snipe and witness woodcock arriving on a full moon, which, for many, signals the start of the season in October. Now I have experienced a type of shooting that inspires the hunting instincts perhaps more than other types. Watching an experienced Gun pitting his wits against a wild bird in its natural habitat does stir the blood. But, as everyone has great pride in telling me, each type of quarry demands the highest respect, whether it be grouse, grey partridge, duck, goose or even the humble pigeon.

# PETER BACON'S TOP TIPS FOR SHOOTING SNIPE & WOODCOCK

As in all forms of shooting safety is paramount, the more so perhaps when there are several Guns walking up woodcock or snipe. Know whom you are shooting with and that they are 'safe shots'. Be aware of where the other Guns are in relation to you at all times and use voice contact frequently to ensure there is no room for error on this point.

The secret to sustainable woodcock shooting is to have sufficient undisturbed ground and to shoot it preferably once a season and certainly not more than twice. Therefore, seek to put together a portfolio of grounds so that there is the potential for say, half-a-dozen days shooting over the season, recognising that some will be suitable when conditions are generally wet while others will work only when there is frost. Twenty- to thirty-acre packages are preferable to large blocks of woodland. It is important to have good fencing if there are sheep or deer or other hooves in the vicinity.

The best type of ground for woodcock obviously is woodland, comprising a mixture of laurel, rhododendron, hazel, willow and plenty of 'dry-lying' on the woodland floor including bracken and bramble and other dense ground cover. Traditionally, where purpose-designed habitats were created these were most usually long rectangular strips, those offering a long sunny edge being favoured and ideally with old pasture adjacent to provide nocturnal feeding opportunities. In addition, sheltered hillsides with good gorse cover are often attractive when conditions have been wet, following periods of heavy rainfall. Woodcock move about depending on the weather, seeking habitats to suit their purpose in varied conditions.

For snipe, the habitat differs from that of woodcock with two main types of bog being favoured – 'green' and 'red' – referring respectively to green marshland and raised heather bogs. Again, as with woodcock, results on one as compared with the other is often down to local conditions at the time of shooting.

Good, close-working dogs are essential both to flush and retrieve. Cockers and springers are most popular in Ireland but there are some walk-up enthusiasts who prefer to use a setter to locate woodcock and snipe.

Always dry off your dog at the end of a day's work and check ears and paws for thorns, burrs etc. Then give a high protein meal.

A day's woodcock or snipe shooting usually involves vigorous exercise, frequently in heavy conditions. The right footwear and clothing are important. Sturdy, waterproof and comfortable boots are essential. A light thornproof outer layer which is completely waterproof is also required, with additional layers underneath as required for comfort.

Always have a full change of clothes in your vehicle for the unexpected 'ducking'.

A 20-bore double barrel shotgun with a 28-inch barrel is ideal. Some specialist woodcock shooters, who spend a lot of the season in dense cover, prefer a weapon with a shorter barrel, down to 26 inches. However for most purposes the less specialised firearm will be more than adequate.

Fibre cartridges of 26–30gm will be adequate. Always pick up spent cartridges.

Remember what the day is about – enjoyment! – in the company of like-minded friends, who can appreciate the privilege of being able to hunt these most elusive of game-birds.

# 8

# PIGEONS

PIGEON SHOOTING SEASON
365 DAYS A YEAR!

# A DAY OUT WITH WILL GARFIT

Ask any shoot enthusiast about pigeon shooting and one name is mentioned with such reverence that I knew if I was to learn anything about the sport I needed to talk to him. Will Garfit, mentored by that late, great pigeon-shooting man Major Archie Coats, has been shooting woodpigeons all his life and spends around sixty days a year in pursuit of these wily agricultural pests. He was kind enough to invite me to his home in Cambridgeshire to experience a day's pigeon decoying.

On the journey down, I was trying to visualise what he might look like and I imagined a round face, slightly plump and dark hair. I was late, getting lost and with a meeting in Yorkshire that evening I was feeling pressured – and beginning to wonder if writing a book about shooting was such a good idea. However, such is the power of a welcoming smile... Will Garfit doesn't look anything like the picture I had conjured up.. He is good-looking, utterly charming and, for the record, played guitar with friends from Cambridge Art School who were later to become Pink Floyd.

We had a quick cup of coffee with his wife, Gina, at the beautiful Georgian rectory which he has called home for more than fifty years, in fact since he was twelve years old. Will's coffee mug is emblazoned with the words 'Think Like a Pigeon' – an aphorism often quoted by Archie Coats. Will showed me where he had catapulted his first pigeon on the front lawn, which was soon dispatched by his Jack Russell terrier, Pincher. Will and Gina are both artists and met at the Byam Shaw School of Art. Sitting in the kitchen with them I have to ask how often they eat pigeon. Will's eyes widen, probably in disbelief that I need to ask the question, and tells me, 'all the time, because you can shoot pigeons three hundred and sixty-five days a year'. His remark reminded me of Harry Ansell whom I met on John Dodd's grouse moor and who thought nothing of eating grouse morning, noon and night. I daresay there aren't many ways that Gina hasn't dished up a pigeon.

Coffee finished and we were off, with more energy than you could whip up out of a dust storm in a stubble field. With Will's six-year-old golden retriever, Scott, in the back of the car we headed straight for a farm near Royston, Hertfordshire. Stan Smith, the farmer, had been in touch with Will to ask him to sort out the escalating pigeon population that was hell-bent on destroying his crops. It is likely that there are an incredible fifteen to twenty million woodpigeons in the UK, all breeding furiously, at least twice every summer. BASC estimate that around a third of the increasing population are shot by more than 200,000 people. So we're not alone. Stan and I shared a common concern for the damage pigeons can do to property: for him it was woodpigeons devouring his crops, while for us at the castle, excrement from feral pigeons rots the lead on the roof. But Will has nothing but respect for his quarry, having studied pigeons for a lifetime, and argues that by understanding how they think you get a much bigger kick out of shooting them because you have to match their tenacity. And they are much cleverer than they seem.

We meet another friend of Will's, AC, who shoots even more pigeons than Will and appears totally unhindered by the fact that he has only one leg. AC brings out the rope bangers, flags and all sorts of bits and bobs to assist the day and off we drive to build a hide in a hedge. In the car Will explains how his friendship with AC has developed from a shared passion for pigeons. (I am tempted to say they are birds of a feather but I could be lambasted for either the cliché or for the pun – so I don't!) The decoys are dead pigeons hoisted on sticks and motorised decoying contraptions. Carefully positioned, they have been set up in a horseshoe shape in front of the hide to act as a landing strip for greedy pigeons eager to join their mates for a tasty feed. The weather, wind direction and flight-lines – the pigeon's routes – have all been taken into account. Fieldcraft requires reconnaissance and experience to manoeuvre the pigeons to the exact spot where you are going to shoot. And patience of course.

I cosy up all hugger-mugger with Will in his hide made of nylon leaves in netting, covered with elder suckers and other foliage; we sit on whirly secretaries' chairs. Everything is well-camouflaged and the sun shines as we wait. My earlier stress is completely forgotten. We've got coffee, salami sandwiches and chocolate to distract us but but Will is on full alert for a sighting. In the summer he'll bring a radio and listen to the cricket as it doesn't put off the pigeons. However, they can see very well and will spot even a slight move-ment a mile away. The secret is to be still, learn to read the flight of the bird and strike at the exact moment of

killability when birds are within fifty yards of the hide.

Will has been shooting with his trusted side-by-side shotgun all his adult life and before that with his .410. But modern fast cartridges are hard on old guns and now he uses a Kemen KM4 over-and-under that he bought second-hand from Mike Yardley, the gun specialist in Essex. Mike claims the latest Kemen guns are some of the finest in the world. They are a lot cheaper, too, than some you can buy, which include a hefty premium for exquisite finishes and engraving. The shooting qualities of this humbler model are as good as the best.

Will shoots pigeons between fifty and sixty days a year and he thinks over the last ten years he has probably shot an average of 100 birds in a day. He shot 300 a few days before my visit in the field behind his house.

Although there is no closed season, spring through to late summer is the best time for pigeon shooting and a stubble field of harvested rape is arguably the best proposition of all. Crops, especially oil seed rape, are magnets to pigeons and farmers are usually very happy to allow responsible shooters on to their land to reduce the numbers.

So here we are, sitting still on our twizzly office chairs, radio contact is live with AC, but as yet there is nothing to report and we just wait. Will tells me about his mentor, Archie Coats, whom he credits with his passion for the sport. (It's an odd coincidence: with only one leg and the initials AC there is a bit of history repeating itself here, with AC out in the field on reconnaissance.) Archie was a professional in all aspects of pigeon shooting and a brilliant shot who seldom missed, shooting with total precision every time. Wild birds and particularly pigeons are testing for any Gun and when they finally make an appearance in front of our hide it's all vim and vigour.

The pigeons approach on their favoured flightline and as each one appears in range, Will plucks them from the sky. He makes it look so easy and you have to remind yourself that it is not. With a wingspan of about two feet and an erratic flight pattern they are very hard to hit and it's a privilege to witness such skill. Scott the dog finally has his chance to prove his moxie too and he expertly retrieves every bird. Every shot was clicked and the tally for the day is sixty. Everything Will has shot will be eaten. He takes a few for himself, as do I, and the rest will go to the local game-dealer for thirty pence each.

*Above. Setting up the Pigeon Magnet, a marvellous motorised decoying contraption that adds movement to a decoy pattern.*

*Left. Will Garfit with Scott, his retriever.*

*Camouflage is a key element in pigeon shooting.*

# A CHANCE MEETING WITH A YOUNG PIGEON-SHOOTING ENTHUSIAST

With my eyes opened to the joys of pigeon decoying I was ready to try it at home. I thought too how much our shooting-mad sons could benefit from learning about reconnaissance and fieldcraft through pigeon shooting, especially now that they have tried goose flighting. Both are very keen to understand more about the countryside and accept that if they want to shoot they have to do their fair share of beating for the keepers in the school holidays. By chance, I met a charming young man, James Ballard, at a late cricket match on our Knipton ground, who more than convinced me that pigeon shooting is an ideal activity for insatiably enthusiastic teenagers. He had this to say:

'I was lucky enough to meet a mad-keen pigeon enthusiast, Tony Davis, when I was nine years old. He had worked for the NFU and was a member of our family's Suffolk shooting syndicate and also, as I found out later, a former protégé of Archie Coats. Tony was always talking about how much he loved pigeon shooting. Being so young I had no idea what he was really on about and I badgered him with endless questions until he agreed to take me with him one day.

'I'll never forget the excitement. We shot eighty-nine pigeons on a field of spring crops and all I wanted was to do it all over again. I spent every school holiday and most weekends in a pigeon hide. My shooting was improving and I was slowly starting to learn the ropes of decoying pigeons. By the time I was thirteen, I was pigeon shooting up to three times a week with Tony who, luckily for me, had retired from work. He would pick me up and we'd drive round to do some reconnaissance and plan where to go for the next day. I soon learnt how much there was to pigeon shooting: flight lines, feeding patterns, crop preferences, decoying tactics, wind direction, weather, hide-building, hide safety – even the best way to shoot the bird was all being shown to me. I was lucky; Tony had

some fantastic areas to shoot over due to his connections with farmers through the NFU. Suffolk is a real hotspot!

'Tony was also introducing me to local farmers and landowners and I was recognising how important it is to respect the land and farmers' fields. It pays if you want to shoot there again. In the winter we have to fit in with estates' partridge and pheasant shoots but in our part of Suffolk, near Bury St Edmunds, a lot of land is planted with oil seed rape and fields are often poisoned with birds.

'When I was seventeen, Tony emigrated to Australia but he left me a huge acreage of land for pigeon shooting through his long list of farming contacts. Until I passed my driving test I had to rely on my parents or anyone who was willing to take me to a field, which limited my reconnaissance and the subsequent success – or lack of success – of some days' shooting. Tony visited two summers ago and we had three great days out shooting together. I could drive by then and it was my turn to take him out and we shot three hundred and ninety pigeons over three separate days. Now I am at university there is still plenty of time for pigeon decoying in the holidays. There seems to be an increase in pigeon numbers in this area since I started nearly ten years ago. Bag numbers seem to be good, however like any other pigeon shooter, some days it works, some days it doesn't!'

# PIGEON FLIGHTING AT BELVOIR

Within days of meeting James Ballard, our son Hugo and his friend Freddie had set up a hide in a suitable position on a field with special friend and top Belvoir ferreting man, Clive Tinkler. Every Sunday morning for the last five years he has come to take the boys ferreting and when they return it's always difficult to tell who has enjoyed it more, as he flashes his big, gold-toothed smile and listens to the boys tell us about the rabbits they have caught. We have all learned so much about the country-side from him and he's usually got plenty to tell us about his home life too. Clive leads a sort of double life: one at Belvoir and the other in the centre of Nottingham. He

*Above*
*Clive Tinkler positioning the*
*pigeon decoys at Belvoir.*

dead. Amazing. What's more amazing is that it was Hugo who shot them! Suddenly he is tuned in and looks quite the expert, peering over the hide for more targets. Poor Freddie looks rather bored but then pigeons start pouring down the flight-line and for two hours we completely lost track of time until all was quiet again.

Five very happy people had twenty pigeons in the bag to show for their efforts and it was time to walk back to the castle and think about how best to cook them.

David's aunt, Lady Ursula D'Abo, a very young ninety-five-year-old, was staying with us for the weekend and we all sat down for a pigeon supper with Clive. I wasn't quite sure if the chemistry between my dinner companions would work but I needn't have worried. The conversation and the laughs inevitably centred on rabbits and pigeons, but we also covered the problems of inner cities (Aunt Ursie lives in London), the war and all the ways rabbit was cooked up to feed everyone during rationing. The chat didn't flag for a second.

# ROOST SHOOTING IN THE FENS

All I needed to experience now was roost shooting, which doesn't really start until February after the pheasant and partridge season is over. As the name suggests, this is about shooting pigeons on their way to roost for the night from a well-camouflaged spot in woodland. Trying to fit this in before our mid- December deadline was difficult but we were lucky. The weather was right, all the leaves had blown off the trees, and a special invitation from Phil Wrisdale, aka Wris, via his friend, Phil Burtt, to visit his Fenland farm was about to satisfy my curiosity.

Wris's farm is in the flat, nutrient-rich landscape of the East Fen in Lincolnshire. Making our way along the drive to his farmhouse, we see hundreds of pigeons flying over a wood called Pool Decoy. It was to this wood that Phil Burtt brought his friend and fellow *Fieldsports* magazine columnist, Lord James Percy, for an afternoon of pigeon shooting with Wris in 2009. James shot ninety-seven pigeons in about two hours and he said it was one of the best afternoons of his life. As pigeon roost shooting is second only to grouse shooting on James's list of favourite pastimes, I am pretty sure that I am about to see something quite special. We were a bit late arriving and with an eye on the fading light, there was no time to waste. Our first stop is a thirty-acre wood called the

*Above*
*Setting up the hide*
*with Clive Tinkler*

*Below*
*Clive explaining*
*the flight line.*

has never moved from the street where he lives with his family and he grows his vegetables on an allotment. He shudders at the depravity of some of the local residents who, like many others in our inner cities, are subject to regular police raids to arrest drug dealers, prostitutes and other criminals.

As well as ferreting, Clive loves pigeon shooting. He has come along to introduce the boys to pigeon flighting. The hide he and the boys built admittedly did not quite have the same finesse as Will and AC's, but hopefully it would be just as effective. Hugo and Freddie placed the decoys out, about thirty metres away from the hide as instructed.

As we waited we sat on crates with a picnic, and listened to Clive's stories. We heard about his mother's pigeon pie, her roasted pigeon and the day the pigeon got away – I forget where from. These were just some of the nuggets that kept us all entertained: we could have waited for hours and the time would still have passed in a flash. Guns were at the ready when, seemingly out of nowhere, the pigeons arrive. Bang, bang, and two are

*Above*
*Counting the quarry*

*Above*
*Returning from the roost*

Deeps, so named because prior to the early 1800s, when this area of fen was drained, it was a deep mere (freshwater lake). We are ushered out of the vehicles at speed, hats and coats secured to keep the rain out, sacks in hand for our quarry, and we follow Wris to a favoured spot in the woods. Reconnaissance every evening for the last seven days has prepared him well. But before we can witness the rewards of his labours he explains how much damage pigeons can do to his crops, especially sprouts, broccoli and cauliflower. If left unchecked they would eat their way through countless acres of produce. But numbers of pigeons in this area have dwindled over the last ten years. Winter vegetables seem to be less popular these days and so less of them are grown, reducing the amount of a once valuable pigeon food source. Added to which, these birds are also extremely partial to oil seed rape, which has become so popular with farmers across the country. This explains why pigeon numbers have increased nationally but reduced in the Fens.

Forty years ago thousands and thousands of them would have been flocking to this wood. Apparently, the excrement and feathers were so thick on the ground that you couldn't put your cartridge bag down without it getting covered. When Wris was growing up in the sixties, and then through until the early nineties, he says: 'If the wind was strong enough and in the right direction, you could stand in a dyke – between two woods – and shoot at literally thousands of pigeons. They would come in with grouse-like speed for up to two hours.' The glory days seem to have passed: today there are merely hundreds and hundreds. Also this year has been a bumper season for acorns, another pigeon delicacy, and Wris believes a lot of birds are choosing to roost in oak plantations nearby instead of his oak-free woods.

For my lesson in pigeon roosting, Wris leaves me with Phil and Spot, his Jack Russell-retriever, in the corner of the wood in a camouflaged hide. I'm told to sit still and not move a muscle. There is barely time for Phil to get his gun out of its sleeve before the pigeons appear in a clearing high up between the trees. If they see a mere flicker of movement they will jink and twist away.

The next forty minutes went in a flash. This sport is so gripping. I can see why anyone who loves the unpredictable trajectory of a grouse will want to shoot pigeons – the action is frenzied. Phil fires several shots and dead birds start to tumble through the trees to the ground. My loading requirements are tested to the full and there is no time for fumbling or cross words. After about half-an-hour we hear the call of a wild pheasant roosting nearby. Phil explains that crows and jackdaws are the last birds to roost and when you hear them you know time is running out. But for the moment there is still a little time left and as we listen to Wris's shots coming from another wood nearby we carry on.

By 3.45pm, on this damp December afternoon, the dusk is darkening and it is time to pick up. Spot had been busy retrieving throughout and had his nose straight onto the remaining birds as I searched for more a bit further afield. Then we caught up with Wris who, with his two beautiful black labs, had picked up plenty too. I felt really charged from such intense activity but my companions remind me that it isn't like the old days. Phil remembers shooting in these woods with his father, Dennis, in the 1980s, and having to run back to the farmhouse twice for more cartridges. Once, they shot 320 pigeons in two hours. Today Phil managed thirty but still had a great evening's sport in under threequarters of an hour.

Pigeon shooting has really opened my eyes. Running a commercial shoot as we do at Belvoir, I had lost sight of the simple joys of this type of hunter-gathering. Will Garfit showed me the pleasure that can come from truly understanding fieldcraft and reconnaissance and I can see that for anyone of any age, with the inclination and the opportunity, pigeon shooting could become addictive. The expressions on my sons' faces as they made their hide and learnt about flight-lines and so on were just as excited as they had been when they were pulling the trigger – and that is so important.

## WILL GARFIT'S TOP TIPS FOR PIGEON SHOOTING

Careful reconnaissance is vital, to find the field where pigeons are feeding. Select the right place for a hide and the right time of day to optimise your sport.

Make a good hide to blend in with surroundings and dress in camouflage.

Use dead birds as decoys.

Keep still in the hide or pigeons will see you and jink away, offering only difficult shots.

Learn to read the flight of a bird and when in range select the moment of maximum killability to shoot.

As with any target with a shotgun – shoot where it is going, not where it's been!

Obviously make sure you have permission from the farmer before you even start reconnaissance work.

Don't get caught out with not enough cartridges. Take as many as you can carry. Also take a hessian sack for quarry and cartridges.

When roost shooting, try and pick up the birds as you shoot them, if possible with a dog.

(See Will's book *Will's Pigeon Shooting* also published by Quiller.)

# 9
# COOKING YOUR GAME

How strange that anyone should kill game and not eat it. Game meat is versatile, very low in fat and utterly delicious. To be fair I don't think there are that many people who don't eat what they have shot and taken home. It was an absolute rule when I was growing up that anyone who brought birds back home had to pluck, dress and cook them themselves – although as I recall I seemed to get lumbered with most of the plucking!

An enormous amount of attention has been given to game meat recently. Recipes are being promoted in magazines and weekend newspaper supplements, restaurants are pushing local produce and game, whilst the Countryside Alliance's Game-To-Eat campaign has had excellent results. The fact that celebrity television chefs are cooking game does more for the game trade than anything else, according to our local butcher.

Dylan Williams, from The Royal Berkshire Shooting School, helped me to run a charity clay shoot at Belvoir and also advised me about our shoot shop. When I told him I was writing a book about shooting, he insisted that I should meet Mike Robinson. Mike owns, runs and cooks for an outside catering business, The Pot Kiln Anywhere, owns The Pot Kiln pub in Berkshire plus The Mike Robinson Game & Wild Food cookery school nearby, and co-owns the Harwood Arms in Fulham – the only pub in London with a Michelin star. He is a wild food expert, passionate about game, which he cooks regularly on his hugely successful programme for ITV, *Countrywise Kitchen.*

So we invited Mike to stay at Belvoir after a shoot. He loves history, fishing, shooting – particularly stalking – and food, all pretty good qualifications for a stay with the Manners family. For me, though, there was the worry about what to give a top chef for dinner. Our chef, Lionel, had made a really good boeuf bourguignon but hadn't really catered for extra guests. There was actually precious little in the kitchen with which to conjure up a decent dinner. Of course that was my fault, but how embarrassing. Just as I was about to suggest going out to a local restaurant someone mentioned that we had a brace of grouse knocking about somewhere. If I'm honest I have to admit that I have never really enjoyed eating grouse: too strong, too pink and too gamey. For me, grouse was definitely an acquired taste. But David kept throwing surreptitious glances at me with a pained and hungry expression on his face.

I needn't have worried about the menu. Once a chef, always a chef and a masterful celebrity chef at

that. Mike wasn't going to turn down an opportunity to prove his mettle with a brace of well-hung grouse. He rolled up his sleeves and took over. He required a roasting tin, a wire rack and a log, apparently to make a smoker. Oh God, then he asked me to pluck the grouse – not that I mind normally, but these two were high, very high. I fumbled about for what felt like an eternity, with feathers and flesh stuck up my nails and seemingly getting nowhere. As for the smell… hmmm. I wouldn't last long as a kitchen apprentice.

Finally Mike saved me from my humiliation and showed me, with lightning dexterity, how to strip a breast from a carcass without having to remove a single feather. Then he covered the breasts with a generous amount of rock salt and placed them in the 'smoker' over the heat. After seven minutes we had the most delicious starter of smoked grouse breast on a pile of dressed salad. Our paupers' portions of melt-in-the-mouth bourguignon were now sufficient and everything was perfect.

After dinner David took Mike on a guided tour of the castle, pointing out the many links with military history – including the gruesome tools used to amputate Lord Robert Manners's leg when he was on board HMS *Resolution* in 1782. The two of them discussed one gory battle after another with obvious relish. Allied to his passion for the countryside and game cookery, we had found the ideal man to help with the book's recipes. Thank you, Dylan!

A lunch invitation followed, to visit Mike at his premises at The Pot Kiln in Berkshire. I met Mike's parents and Alan Haywood, the local butcher, a gentle countryman who loves deer-stalking with Mike. He has been the chef's mentor and taught him many of his butchery skills. Lunch was a feast of game dishes all exquisitely executed and bursting with intense flavours. I defy anyone not to like game when it is cooked properly. Even our children are complete converts.

Mike talks me through the whole process of how he chooses game from the dealer: right season, fresh, plump and not over-shot. We visit Alan's premises and the abattoir, and I am learning that food isn't just about cooking. You must understand its provenance, judge its quality and freshness, and have complete trust in your suppliers.

Finally we go to the *Countrywise Kitchen,* which is used for filming, and during the rest of the afternoon Mike showed me how to make the six amazingly simple but utterly delicious dishes that he has picked for the book.

*Above*
*With Mike Robinson and his*
*ex-wife and business partner,*
*Katie Robinson.*

# RECIPES BY MIKE ROBINSON

'As a chef whose whole working life is centred around game and wild food, the field sports and shooting industry is not just important, but crucial! I truly believe that shooting has been the making of much of our fabulous countryside, and is its future. The sport provides us with employment, conservation and ingredients, but is often misunderstood. To me, the only justification for shooting large numbers of game birds is that we eat them. Not tentatively, but with gusto!

In the last seven years I have seen the attitude to game change radically in this country. Pheasants, partridges, pigeons and grouse are now the mainstay of many restaurant menus, and are quite rightly regarded as some of the finest ingredients with which we can work.

I don't just love cooking game, I love eating it too, so when I received a call from Emma telling me she was trying to promote shooting and game meat, I was honoured to supply a few of my favourite home recipes for her book.

The key to cooking game is to understand it. This is not reared chicken – we are talking free-range and nervous! There is very little fat and lots of protein in the meat – this is what makes it so good for us to eat. There are two overriding issues that put people off this wonderful meat. One is over-hanging – smelly meat is just not acceptable to most folks these days as our taste buds are not used to it. The other is overcooking.

When meat such as pheasant is slightly overcooked, the fibres become very noticeable and the meat becomes dry and stringy. Reduce your cooking time; increase the resting time; and the end result will be brilliant. Please try these little recipes, they are all quick and easy, and have given me much pleasure over the years. Feel free to change things around too: a recipe is only a guide, after all.'

# PHEASANT KIEV

## FOR THE BUTTER
*1 small bunch of basil, 1 small bunch of oregano, 1 small bunch of parsley, 6 cloves of garlic, the zest of 1 lemon, 1 block (250g) butter*

## FOR THE KIEVS
*4 pheasant breasts, 2 eggs, 200mls milk, 250g plain flour, 250g white breadcrumbs, (or for a really crispy topping, try and find Japanese Panko breadcrumbs, available in large supermarkets and Asian food stores) 2 litres vegetable oil, 1 tsp sea salt, black pepper*

Serves 4

*My first recipe is fantastically simple and very retro: Pheasant Kiev. This is without doubt my favourite way of cooking a pheasant breast and gives an amazing result. The armour of breadcrumbs seals in all the juices and the honking garlic and herb butter within is awesome. This will be the juiciest, quickest pheasant dish ever, and can be prepared in advance. Brilliant as part of a classy dinner or served to the kids in front of the telly, this is a real winner.*

Start by making the butter. Put the roughly chopped herbs, lemon zest and garlic into a food processor and whizz with the butter until you have a smooth, smelly green paste. Put the resulting mixture into a piping bag, and keep it in a warm place, so the butter does not harden.

Remove the skin from the pheasant breasts. Then, inserting a small knife into the thick end of the breast, open up a 2- to 3-inch pocket in the meat. Pipe in a good tablespoonful of the butter mix, repeat with the other breasts, then cover and put in the fridge to set.

Beat the eggs and milk together and pour into a shallow dish. Season the flour and put it in a separate dish and the breadcrumbs in another, so that you have three dishes side by side: flour in one, then the egg mix, then the breadcrumbs. Coat the breasts with the seasoned flour, dip them on both sides in the egg wash, then transfer to the breadcrumbs. Coat completely with breadcrumbs, return to the egg wash and crumb them a second time. This gives them complete protection from the oil.

Heat the oil in a deep pan, or in your deep fryer, to 180°C. Deep fry for 6 minutes until golden brown. Remove, drain on a rack and leave to rest for 3 or 4 minutes.

How you serve the Kievs is up to you, but watercress goes well with them, as does sautéed spinach. Crisp dry white wine is essential.

# PARTRIDGE SALTIMBOCCA WITH PEAS AND CREAM

Serves 4

*This is a really classy, easy and elegant dish that is perfect for an autumnal dinner. It requires a little advance preparation but the end result is totally worth it. The French partridge is the most perfectly designed culinary game bird, and really mild and delicious in flavour. In this recipe, we are wrapping the breasts in sage and prosciutto, and serving them with a bowl of mustardy peas in cream and cider – unbeatable.*

Preheat your oven to 200°C/Fan 180°C/400°F/Gas mark 6.

Start by laying a sage leaf on to each breast, then wrap each one in half a slice of Parma ham (a whole slice if you are feeling flush!). Season well with sea salt (Maldon or similar) and black pepper. Find a good big sauté pan and melt half the butter. Sear the birds breast side down in the foaming butter, spooning it over them as they cook. Do not turn for two minutes. Turn over carefully and lay on a roasting tray. Pop them into the pre-heated oven for 7 minutes.

Meanwhile, using the same pan, add the rest of the butter, the finely chopped shallots and the finely chopped sage and soften for 2 minutes. Add the peas and the mustard. Pour in a glass of cider and reduce it by half, then add the cream. Cook until rich and season to taste.

The partridges need to rest for 5 minutes after roasting, so time the peas accordingly. Serve in a bowl with 1–2 partridge breasts per person. I would drink rosé with this dish.

*8 partridge breasts, 8 fresh sage leaves, 4 slices Parma ham, sea salt, black pepper, 100g butter, 2 shallots, 6 sage leaves, 250g frozen peas, 1 tbsp wholegrain mustard, a glassful of good cider, 100mls double cream*

# PHEASANT OR PARTRIDGE IN ROSEMARY, WHITE WINE AND LEMON

Serves 4

*This is a really quick at-home supper and always works a treat. Takes no more than 30 minutes and is never dry!*

Take the halved birds and cut them again between the breast and thigh portions. Pop them in a big freezer bag and add the oil, bruised rosemary and squashed garlic, as well as the quartered lemons. Leave for at least an hour or overnight to marinade. Then get a big oven pan on the heat and also preheat the oven to 200°C/Fan 180°C/400°F/Gas mark 6. Pour the contents of the bag into the pan and fry until the meat is golden. Pour in the wine and season well. Pop the pan into the oven for 20 minutes for pheasants or 15 minutes for partridges. Remove from the oven. Allow to rest for 5 minutes then serve with salad and fried potatoes.

*2 hen pheasants, cut in half down the breast bone*
*or*
*4 partridges, prepared the same way, 100mls of really good extra virgin olive oil,*
*6 sprigs of rosemary, 12 unpeeled cloves of garlic, 2 lemons, quartered, 2 glasses of white wine,*
*sea salt and black pepper*

# ROAST MALLARD CROWN WITH SOY AND HONEY

Serves 4

*Mallard, and indeed wigeon, teal and all our other wild ducks are quite simply amazing eating. I have huge admiration for the masochists of the shooting world, the wildfowlers. This hardy breed will endure conditions of staggering discomfort to shoot these wonderful birds, and do great conservation work in the process.*

*This method of cooking the ducks ensures a delicate pink result, and the soy and honey give it a really complementary Asian slant.*

Preheat the oven to 200°C/Fan 180°C/400°F/Gas mark 6. Mix the soy, honey and lime juice together, then add in the seasoning and five-spice. Paint the crown with this mix and sear, breast side down, in a heavy pan in the vegetable oil. Place the crowns in the oven for 18 minutes (less for a smaller duck). After the first 10 minutes add the legs. Remove the duck crowns and legs; paint them with some more marinade and rest for 10 minutes, at least! Carve the breasts from the crowns in one piece – they will be pink and juicy. Then carve across the grain into 5 or 6 slices each and serve on well-spiced red cabbage.

*2 mallard crowns (the breast plates with the breasts still attached), 1 tbsp dark soy sauce*
*1 tbsp honey juice of 1 lime, salt and szechuan pepper, 1 tsp five-spice powder, 2 tbsp vegetable oil*

# OLD-FASHIONED ROAST WOODCOCK

Serves 2

*The woodcock is our most iconic gamebird, and the highlight of every gameshooter's shooting year. Hard to shoot, unpredictable and mind-blowingly delicious, I really love the woodcock. This is the original way to cook them and is not for the faint-hearted, but the method pays this astonishing bird great respect and that is really important.*

*The guts of the woodcock are always empty when they take off, so traditionally are cooked in the bird. Personally I like to remove them before cooking and use them later.*

Preheat the oven to 200°C/Fan 180°C/400°F/Gas mark 6. Remove the guts from the woodcock, reserving them in a bowl. Rub the birds with half the butter and brown really well in a pan for 2 or 3 minutes. Spoon the butter over the birds continuously to get a really good colour. Place the birds on the toast and lay the bacon over their breasts. Roast in the oven for 16 minutes, then remove and rest. While the birds are resting, melt the remainder of the butter in a small pan. Finely chop the guts and sauté for 2 minutes. Add the chicken livers and fry for another 2 minutes. Add the cognac and the cream, then blitz with a hand blender into a pâté. Season and add the thyme leaves. Spoon the pâté onto the toast. Remove the breasts and carve them, do the same with the legs. Then split the skull and beak lengthways. Serve with the rich sauce and baby vegetables, being sure to give your guests a teaspoon for the brains!

*2 woodcock, plucked, heads left on, 100g butter, 2 pieces of toast, 2 thick slices of smoked bacon, 2 chicken livers, 2 tbsp double cream, a splash of cognac, salt and black pepper, 2 sprigs of thyme*

# SMOKED GROUSE

### Serves 4 as a starter

*This is a great way to serve an old grouse, and smoking really complements the flavour of this rich, strong bird. It is ridiculously easy to do and needs only a few ingredients.*

*You will need a deep roasting tin that is strongly made, a trivet (wire rack) and a handful of oak chippings, which you can buy from any kitchen shop. The day I did this dish at Belvoir I grated an oak log from the fire basket, so there is no excuse for not doing it! A microplane grater is very useful for this.*

Remove the grouse breasts and lay them on a board. Sprinkle liberally with sea salt and pepper. Leave for 1 hour to cure a little – this will draw out some of the blood and moisture and allow the smoke to penetrate. After 1 hour, wash off the cure and pat the breasts dry. Lay the chippings in the bottom of the roasting tin and put the trivet on top. Lay the grouse breasts on the trivet and cover the whole thing with a double layer of foil, which must be tightly folded over the edges to create a seal.

Put the oven dish on the hob over a medium heat. Leave to cook for 10 minutes – the inside of the tin will act like a smoky oven. Ideally you want to cook the grouse until they are cooked in texture but still pink all the way through.

I like to serve these warm in a salad with crisp bacon and goat's cheese, and peppery salad leaves.

Of course, you can cook pheasant and partridge, or even duck, in the same way.

*2 or more grouse, 2 tbsp coarse sea salt, 1 tsp black pepper, 2 tbsp oak chippings, a wire trivet, 2 sheets of thick tinfoil*

10

I have learnt more about game, about shooting and about the different quarry species in a few months than I would ever have thought possible. From my first day on a grouse moor in August to the two days I spent back in Powys to shoot at Stanage and at home with my family before Christmas, I have scoured over a hundred documents, letters, gamebooks and pictures in Belvoir's archives to gain a historical perspective; travelled over 2,500 miles by car, plane and boat to visit more than twenty shoots; and have met more than five hundred people who either run shoots, help out on them or actually pull the trigger.

I believe that our shooting heritage may always be perceived as a controversial paradox. However I have also come to realise that it is an industry that can only thrive on a proper respect for wildlife and habitat – and evidence of that respect I have seen absolutely everywhere that I have visited. The successful development of the sport is being driven by passionate individuals who are totally dedicated to what they do, whilst always being open to new ideas in terms of habitat management and conservation.

Viewed from my own perspective at Belvoir, the 5th Duke of Rutland should be given much of the credit for shaping the estate and developing the shoot that we know today. His personal 'green and pleasant land' is no different in essence now from the time when his contemporary William Blake wrote those words in the early 1800s when the estate was being developed. Who knows what lies ahead in the next two hundred years but I hope shooting will still be as vital to the biodiversity and sustainability of the estate as it ever was.

Nowadays we try to provide maximum shooting entertainment for our guests in a professional but relaxed way: their enjoyment is of huge importance to us, and of course to our reputation and success. That

enjoyment can be enhanced, as I have discovered, by offering more than just the shooting itself.

# THE BELVOIR SHOP

As more and more shooting parties pass through our doors I am frequently asked about what to wear and what to shoot with. I have Phil O'Brien, my former business manager, to thank for showing me how to manage my energy, time and arguably harebrained ideas, which led to the birth of both the shoot shop and our own shotgun. He joined our team in 2009 to help us make the most of this wonderful estate. Sitting in my office one afternoon, and after much mulling, he suggested that the business would fair much better if we concentrated our efforts on the shoot, perhaps even opening a shoot shop. That would give our Guns a one-stop opportunity to buy cartridges, clothes, books and other shooting paraphernalia, or even to buy a gun. The idea would mean closing the castle to the public during the winter season, a difficult decision, and it was hard to imagine having to cancel our traditional Christmas events. But after talking to our

*Shoot lunch in the State Dining Room at Belvoir with family and friends.*

*Belvoir's shoot shop.*

Guns and travelling to sporting trade fairs in America, Russia, South America and Dubai, I learnt that many people, particularly international visitors, really like the idea of a one-stop-shop on a shoot.

We looked at all the shoot clothing on the market and decided to stock mostly Really Wild Clothing and Barbour. Then there are all the extras: gloves, socks, ear defenders, smart drinks boxes, fur accessories, greetings cards, children's clothes, hats – you name it.

We finally opened for business in November 2011 with a huge party with friend Liz Cavell-Taylor, who joined us to launch her new sporting travel company, Field Sports Travel. Our intention was to unite the interests of as many shooting people as possible, both from this country and from abroad.

# THE 'RUTLAND' SHOTGUN

The next idea that we had was to develop and market our own gun. Ideally it would have to be English and a side-by-side, because David is a traditionalist. However a good friend, Louise Nickerson (daughter-in-law of the late Joseph Nickerson and a shot of considerable repute), suggested an over-and-under. The arguments between the supporters of over-and-unders and side-bysides are notorious and I was confused to say the least, so she arranged for me to meet a new gunmaker, James Stewart of Longthorne Guns. He had just produced his first ever gun, an over-and-under, which he launched at the 2010 CLA Game Fair at Blenheim.

James is not a typical gunmaker by trade and in fact he had never made a gun before but had always been fascinated by engineering and shooting. Louise had examined his new gun, the English-made Hesketh, with forensic enthusiasm and was impressed. I had previously talked to a couple of European gunmakers but really liked the concept of an all-English model so we met up at Belvoir to discuss our ideas – which I am delighted to say are coming to fruition!

James's company is a family business. His wife, Elaine, was working in marketing for a firm of mechanical engineers when they met in the early 1980s. Together they started an engineering business in Australia, where they lived for a few years, producing parts for firearms and bicycles for The Australian Institute of

*Above*
*This very early flintlock gun belonging to the 3rd Duke was left to his illegitimate son, Edward Manners, and was later presented to the 9th Duke by Walter Evelyn Manners (Edward's descendant). The inscription reads:*
*'This gun dated 1764 belonged to John, 3rd Duke of Rutland (1696–1779). It was presented to John, 9th Duke of Rutland by Walter Evelyn Manners 1934'.*
*The family collection is soon to acquire a brand new shotgun that we have designed ourselves with Longthorne Guns.*

Sport amongst others. To cut a long story short, they returned to the UK in 1998 and arrived back in Lancashire with five forty-foot containers that held their possessions and their 'factory', and set about making a childhood dream a reality.

The factory is housed in an old farm building that has been used in the past to make parts for Formula One cars and it was there that he produced the Hesketh and where the 'Rutland' shotgun is being developed. Daughter Chloe has great artistic flair and she designed the engraving patterns on the Hesketh; now she has come up with a design for our gun that incorporates elements of the Rutland coat of arms with peacocks on the sidelock plate. A slight oriental touch in the design also reflects some of the Chinese influences on the Regency decoration in some of the castle's rooms. As for the gun itself, after much discussion, it is a true sidelock, over-and-under 12-bore shotgun, incorporating Longthorne solid barrels and all the features expected of a fine English handmade shotgun.

# SHOTGUNS IN GENERAL

Obviously a book like this is not the place to try to give a comprehensive guide to the whole subject of shotguns and their care. I am still learning about all the different choices, barrel length, choke sizes, over-and-under, side-by-side and so on, myself. David, who worked in the arms and armour department at Christie's before we were married, suggested I talk to William Elderkins, from his family's gunsmiths, Elderkins in Spalding, for a proper introduction to guns, which I did. Perhaps his words of wisdom may be of use to others who are novices like me.

Driven game shooting, as we know it today, resulted from the development of the breech-loading gun in the mid-1800s and then towards the end of that century the hammerless and also ejector models appeared. British gun making in that period was hugely innovative with different styles of ejector systems and actions. Top London gunmakers such as Purdey, Boss and Holland & Holland pioneered the development and production of some of the best sidelock ejectors in the world and these have been copied across the globe.

But while London's makers steamed ahead with the finest models on the market for royalty, aristocracy and rich industrialists, the Birmingham trade concentrated on cheaper utility guns. Alongside sidelocks and hammer guns they specialised in the boxlock action, which worked better for wildfowling, rough shooting and pigeon shooting.

By the late 1960s, commercial shoots and local farmers' syndicates opened up shooting to many more people and they wanted to buy a gun over the counter and at an affordable price. European manufacturers were quick to facilitate this and foreign guns started to make an appearance with Spanish side-by-sides, copying our boxlocks and sidelocks, and Italian-produced over-and-unders. The Europeans could produce cheaper, reliable alternatives with advanced technology for the machine-made gun and consequently the hand-made English boxlock was losing favour.

Britain still produces the finest sidelock ejectors and some of the best over-and-unders priced from £70,000 upwards for a bespoke London shotgun. A side-by-side, built to the same standards, will cost slightly less because it requires fewer hours to make. Apparently the mechanics and configuration of an over-and-under requires about 1200 hours' work as opposed to 850–900 hours for a side-by-side. Traditionally the side-by-side has always been the most favoured gun but these days the over-and-under is growing in popularity. Its single sighting plane, which helps beginners, also allows for more measured shooting at long range and it absorbs the recoil well. Which is best for you boils down to personal preference.

Maintenance and servicing can easily be overlooked and as Mr Elderkins comments: 'You can use a gun all season, put it away in February and forget about it until the beginning of the next season. You will have forgotten that the gun didn't eject, misfired or was loose on the last day.' He advises that with older English guns, it is best to have them stripped down and checked over regularly. If a gun has had a lot of hard use, then it should always be oiled and reassembled by a trained, renowned gunsmith. The barrels should always be checked to see whether any dents or bulges have appeared which need removing before the gun is fired again, or extra strain on the steel will build up. If the blueing on the barrels is beginning to wear it should be redone to help stop rust appearing during damp or wet days. During a pre-season service the firing pins should also be checked so there is no 'mushrooming': a term used to describe what happens when the hammer hits the firing pin and causes it to burr, which can cause intermittent misfires. Finally, the firing pins should be checked for cracking or breaks.

Other technical factors that should also be looked at include the springs. English guns are nearly always 'V' springs, evidently they either work or they break and these should be checked too for any cracks, as should the hammer and sears.

Mr Elderkins warns that if a gun's action is loose, it is probably because it needs to be re-jointed. If you carry on using it as it is, it will put extra strain on the gun. There is movement when the explosion occurs from the cartridges, which is three-tons-per-square-inch pressure, and this can cause excessive wear on the action. But a new body pin, or modern techniques of spray welding into the hook of the barrel, will bring the barrels back down tight to the face. If the gun is perfectly tight, i.e. there is no headspace between the chamber and the action, this will help reduce excessive recoil.

As for the appearance of your gun: the woodwork will benefit from a light oiling for optimum maintenance. If lots of marks have appeared and the chequering is getting worn, for the sake of pride of ownership and keeping the value of the gun, it's always worth – every so often – having it stripped down, the marks removed, and then oiled and the chequering re-cut and re-finished.

Maintenance is certainly a worthwhile exercise, but first, unless you have been lucky enough to inherit a gun, you need to buy one. Again, the tips given here are only intended as a brief guide: there is no substitute for doing your own comprehensive research before you invest in such an important purchase.

*Below*
*The over-and-under shotgun is*
*becoming increasingly popular.*

*A good gun is obviously essential for shooting high birds like these.*

# WILLIAM ELDERKIN'S TOP TIPS FOR BUYING A GUN

It can be quite a minefield when it comes to buying a gun: different bores, different barrel lengths, over-and-unders or side-by-sides, so I will try to explain the differences.

---

Most people select a 12 bore for game shooting. This is the most universal gun and can be used with various loads of cartridge; the lighter loads for partridges, grouse and early pheasants, a heavier load if needed for later in the season.

---

People have different ideas on barrel length. One misconception is that the longer the barrel the further the gun will kill, which years ago was the case as black powder and slower burning powders were used in the cartridges, so the longer the barrel the more pressure was built up. These days with cartridges being very quick and powders being virtually instant by implosion, barrel length is less important.

---

The chokes in the gun make the difference on the range. I am personally a fan of improved cylinder and 1/4 choke for most shooting. For later in the season or on the more extreme shoots where birds are driven on the top of valleys, then one could go tighter with chokes. As I always tell customers, putting one pellet in the right place is better than ten pellets in the wrong place!

---

Barrel length is now more of a fashion. During the 1970s the 25-inch barrels with Churchill quick-sighting rib were very popular, being very quick to swing. However, where that can be an advantage, a gun that is quick to swing is also quick to stop, and I feel that more birds can be missed with the gun being stopped than the lead being wrong.

---

The most popular barrel length is 28 inches, which has come to be regarded as the optimum barrel length for game shooting. Over recent years longer barrels have come back into fashion, this being for people who want to shoot the more extreme birds where longer barrels are steadier at swing and give more pointability.

---

As with all these things there is no one particular gun that will suit all. More importantly than barrel length I feel that the fit of the gun is the most important part. Someone can spend thousands of pounds on a gun but if that gun is not shooting where you are looking, the money has been wasted. Everybody is different on stock fit and a good gunmaker would be able to advise on the fit. The best way is to go to a known shooting ground and have a lesson and fitment by one of their coaches. To give an example, if you are a 1/4 inch out at the stock end, that accentuates to approximately 4 to 5 feet out at 30 yards. I feel the easiest way to explain this is that the angle you are out this end gets greater and greater the further you go.

---

20 bores are now very fashionable and these perform as well as a 12 bore with the pattern being not so wide. One has to be more accurate which is part of the challenge of these guns.

---

16 bores have been out of fashion for quite some time because there is now a far bigger selection of 20 bore cartridges on the market. I would say though that they are probably the perfect gun if you are looking for a lighter gun but it will still throw a very good slightly wider pattern.

---

28 bores have begun to appear in the field recently and these show an even smaller pattern. I have seen some very accomplished shots shoot very well with these. However, they use very large load cartridges to counteract the smaller width pattern while giving a longer strain to the pattern.

---

I usually recommend .410s and 28 bores for a youth starting to shoot, or certainly a 28 bore for a lady who is starting to shoot, because it's a light gun with less recoil.

---

Whether to go side-by-side or over-and-under is again down to personal preference. Over recent years the over-and-under has become more fashionable in the field. With the one line to aim down (not that you should be looking at the barrel as it means that you will miss) you see the one line in your peripheral vision, which is certainly easier and more forgiving especially with the longer measured shots. Today most people have their first shot at a clay ground, whereas years ago most people probably went out with their father's side-by-side and shot rabbits.

---

Side-by-sides are still popular and do the job just as well; however, I would say that the side-by-side is for the instinctive shot, whereas the over-and-under may be better for the longer, more measured shot with its different sight picture and more concentration.

---

Basically, find the gun you like in the right price bracket. Make sure you really like the look and feel of it, and make sure the all-important fit is made to the gun. My advice is to buy something that you are going to enjoy and have pride of ownership in.

# POSTSCRIPT

I hope you have enjoyed this season of discovery about shooting as much as I have: it has been a marvellous experience and one that I would not have missed for anything. It has made me so much more appreciative of the many aspects of this wonderful sport of ours and even more aware of the importance of preserving it for future generations. I know that I still have so much more to learn, and what a pleasure it is to anticipate that process.

Emma
Duchess
of Rutland

# ACKNOWLEDGEMENTS

With just under one shooting season to write about my journey of discovery there was absolutely no time to waste and I will be eternally grateful to several key people who have helped me to meet the deadline. Firstly, as always, I have to thank my family, David and our five children – Violet, Alice, Eliza, Charles and Hugo – for their unfailing support and patience while I scrambled to more than twenty shoots in five months. Thanks, too, to my parents, John and Roma Watkins, for helping me to trawl through my childhood recollections of our family shoot.

A special thank you goes to our shoot captain, Phil Burtt, who has introduced me to so many of his friends: they not only invited me to their fabulous shoots but didn't mind me tagging along with notebook, photographer and endless questions. My PA, Megan Turner, has also been unstinting in her administrative efforts; Peter Foden, our archivist, has unearthed endless game books, visitors' books and letters for information about the Belvoir shoot since it started in 1800; and Edward Sparrow found some great statistics in the archives during a day's work experience. Big thanks too to our own shoot staff, past and present, especially former head keeper Ron Wells, who have all obliged me with answers to many a strange question, as have Richard Sanders and Nick Ainscough, our land agents, from Fisher German.

Our photographers, Charlie Sainsbury-Plaice, Rupert Watts, Hannah Stieger-White, Alice Harvey, Max Milligan, Deborah Green and Ger Lawlor have all been brilliant and thrown themselves into the project through wind, rain and shine. Many thanks, too, to Mike Barnes, editor of *Fieldsports* magazine, for his support and help with various chapters; to Jonathan Young, editor of *The Field*, for his wonderful contribution about etiquette; to Amanda Anderson at The Moorland Association for reading through and checking the grouse chapter and Morag Walker at the GWCT. An almighty big thank you each to Brent Pope, Pattie Wilson, Will Garfit and Peter Bacon, all of whom not only gave me so much time on their shoots, but also contributed their top tips, as did William Elderkins for tips on buying a gun. Also thanks to Mike Robinson, who despite wrestling with tight filming schedules for his television programme still produced some delicious recipes for our food chapter.

I am hugely indebted to all the shoots that have welcomed me and all the owners, shoot captains, game keepers, pickers-up, beaters, loaders, chefs, cooks and countless Guns who have contributed to my understanding of their sport. There isn't enough space to mention them all and if I have forgotten anyone, I do apologise, but to John Dodd, Danny Lawson, Wenty Beaumont, Ann and Peter Hood, Robbie Douglas Miller, Geoff Eyres, Dr Adam Smith, Simon Lester, David Ross, Michael Cannon, Richard Johnson, Fiona Robinson, Mark Rennison, the Duke of Northumberland, Gerald and Lizzie Needham, John Pochin, James Goodson, Trevor Ash, Lord Barnard, Lindsay Waddell, Tim Dean, David Boynton, Deborah Green, Joan Hicks, Stephen Partridge-Hicks, Charlie and Lizzy Williams, Jamie Parsons, Alan Campbell, Philip Tidball, John Alexander, Jonathan and Sophie Coltman-Rogers, Bernard and Sarah Taylor, William Davies, Brent Pope, John Cutler, Toby Ward, Patrick Hungerford, Heather MacGregor, Clive Tinkler, Emma Weir, Lucilla Noble, Toby Fichtner-Irvine, Mary MacEwan, Adam Fox-Edwards, David Pilkington, Adrian and Catherine Sweeney, Hazel Bacon, Susan Kellett, Roderick and Helena Perceval, Mike and Penny Tanner, James Ballard, Phil Wrisdale, James Stewart and Dylan Williams – thank you.

Without the quiet determination of my literary agent, Barbara Levy, and the belief in the project from publisher Andrew Johnston, the book would never have got beyond the idea stage. Andrew Bates and Adrian Baker of Tin Can Design, the designers, have wielded their magic and added the polish. Lastly, my thanks to Jane Pruden, who understood what I was trying to achieve from the start and transcribed my thoughts and ramblings into words. Thank you to you all.

# PHOTO CREDITS

All the black and white photographs in Chapter One are from the Belvoir archives.

# INDEX